DWYC
today

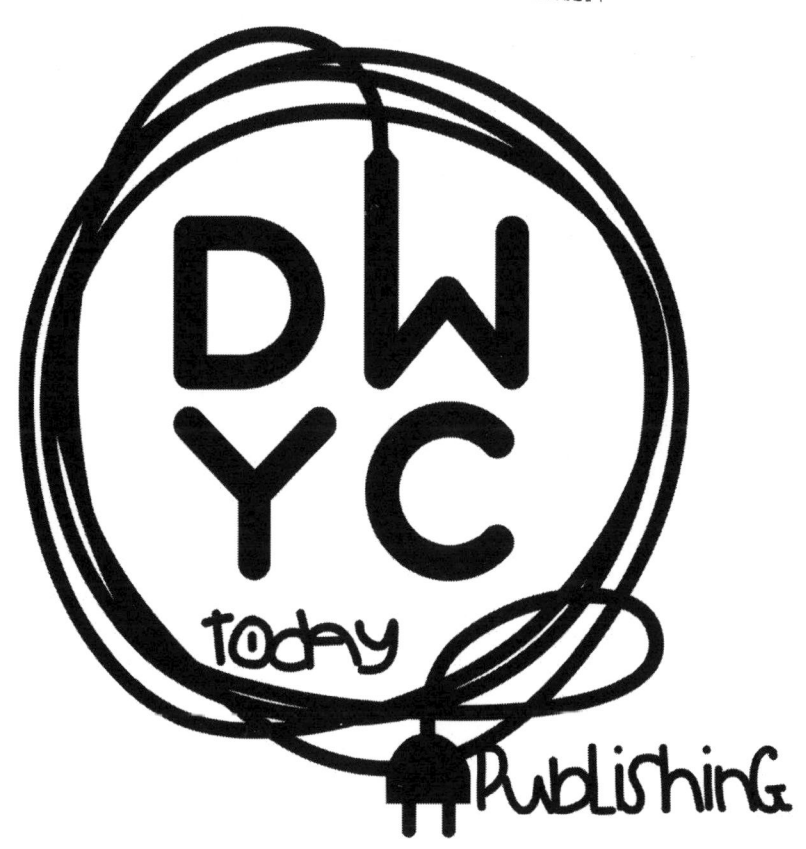

Publishing

A seemingly fictional, non-fiction love story with a psychedelic twist.
Written by Ren Koi and lovingly edited by Lynette Allen

tOGEthER

AN AYAHUASCA EXPERIENCE

REN KOI

With all my love, I dedicate this book to Adele, Lillian, Isobel, and Teddy.

xx

THANKS

I'm very grateful to my parents, my fiancée Adele and my step-children Lillian and Isobel, my dog Teddy, my sponsor Alex M, Al Goodbody, and all my fellows in Twelve Step fellowships, all my family and friends, and all those whose stories contributed to the formation of this book, including: the Pachamama Temple shaman and facilitators, the retreat hosts Mark, Lynette and Livvie, and my ayahuasca 'tribe': Austin, Sam, Natasha, Angela, Lisa, Leanne, Luke, Daran, John, Justus, Amy, Ingrida, Lita and Tim.

PEACE
AND
LOVE

CHAPTERS

0.0 SUFFERING
- 0.1 THE PALACE OF WISDOM
- 0.2 UNIVERSAL ADDICTION
- 0.3 THERE IS AN ANSWER

1.0 PREPARATION
- 1.1 A WALK IN THE WOODS
- 1.2 AMY'S STORY (PART 1)

2.0 CEREMONY
- 2.1 SPIRITUAL MALADY
- 2.2 GUILT AND REMORSE
- 2.3 AMY'S STORY (PART 2)
- 2.4 LOVE, LOVE, LOVE
- 2.5 LEANNE'S STORY
- 2.6 DOWNLOAD

3.0 ILLUMINATION
- 3.1 COSMIC JOKE
- 3.2 ANGELA'S STORY
- 3.3 TRIBE
- 3.4 JESUS, BUDDHA, AND MOSES
- 3.5 LUKE'S STORY

4.0 GOD IS LOVE
- 4.1 THE GOOD
- 4.2 OVERCOMING PAIN

5.0 **REALITY**
5.1 RECONCILIATION
5.2 GOSPEL OF AYAHUASCA

6.0 **LESSONS**
6.1 HUMMINGBIRD
6.2 ROUND TWO

7.0 **ONWARD**
7.1 REIKI
7.2 THE AGE OF TRUTH
7.3 ALL THAT MATTERS

"THE MYSTICS AND THE MADMEN ARE IN THE SAME WATERS BUT THE MYSTICS ARE SWIMMING AND THE MADMEN ARE DROWNING"

– Futurist, Jason Silva

FOREWORD

"Over a decade ago, I sat on my own one night late on my sofa, staring at the TV. Transfixed. Absolutely mesmerised as the BBC filmed Bruce Parry on his TV documentary 'Tribe' taking ayahuasca. They recorded the early part of the ceremony as he took the brew and started to feel its effects. I watched intently as he talked about his journey, what he felt, the depth in his eyes, how he described the effects of this powerful psychedelic brew, as he sat in front of a mud hut in the depths of goodness knows where. I knew at that point that I would never be brave enough to try anything like that but I loved that he did, and I hung on each word as he described the whole experience.

Fast forward almost a decade and I'm sitting on another sofa late at night, in another house, with my 2nd husband, in another life, and he tells me he wants to try ayahuasca. At the time, I didn't link the two experiences together. I claimed I had no idea what it was but as he spoke, I sat in shock. What? Why! Really? My husband wants to do this? You wait til' your nearly 50 before you want to try drugs? Yep. That's what I thought. I'd been well brought up with parents who drummed the NO's of drugs into me, whose fear prevented me from even smoking a cigarette, let alone anything stronger. While my counterparts were exploring getting drunk on vodka and crawling out of their bedroom windows to party, I was studying hard, getting good grades and swimming a mile most mornings. I'd never done anything like this and I had no idea why my husband wanted to either.

His fascination only grew, as did my distress at him wanting to try it. We had conversations, he tried to educate me, I was blinded by my upbringing and I couldn't understand. In September 2016, Mark went for his first ayahuasca ceremony. I cried most of the weekend. And the relief when I heard from him, that he was ok and that he'd had an amazing time, was so overwhelming I cried even more. In fact, I now know that his energy shift from his ayahuasca experience caused me to sink into my own healing crisis – which at the time felt like 'I' was falling apart – when in fact, the foundations of my strength, and my own healing journey, were only just beginning.

I thought now he'd tried ayahuasca and experienced it, that was that. But no. He announced he wanted to make it part of his own spiritual practice, monthly. What? Why! Again... I had no idea. Just no idea. I was so torn between wanting to support my husband in doing what he felt right and simultaneously being so utterly confused; rejecting the idea of ayahuasca as little more than getting high once a month with what he called his 'new family.'

I remember one day saying, "Darling if you really want to do this, I will support you, but don't ever expect me to do it." He didn't. He never asked me to do it or try it. He simply carried on, with his own healing journey and slowly I started to 'feel' the results. I say 'feel' because it's not something you can put your finger on. I can't say with any clarity how he changed, just that he did. And with each time HE drank, I felt as though I had drunk also... I was being pushed to change too... energetically.

7 months after Mark's first cup of ayahuasca, I took mine. As he was becoming whole, as he was growing from the inside – from the very core of himself, I realised more than ever that I wanted to do the same. I had my own hurts and wounds to heal from. On 4th March 2017, I entered my own ayahuasca ceremony. I was very, very nervous. But I knew I had to do it. I wanted to do this. I'd seen such change first hand, I'd heard so many stories of change and healing. And I'd remembered that night nearly a decade before when I'd been struck by Bruce Parry and his first meeting with 'Mother Ayahuasca.' This was my turn. My turn to do something I never in a million years thought I'd be brave enough to do. To look into myself, accept what I saw, and grow from it.

From that next morning, I could honestly look Mark in the eye and say "OK... I get it." For the first time, I started to understand. And I've learned so much since that night. Those early months in my journey were also the beginning of a massive journey Mark and I were to embark on, taking other people through THEIR ayahuasca journeys also. Little did I know at that point, how much ayahuasca, the time spent with her, the time delving into my 'self,' would impact me, or mean to me.

Over the course of the following 2 years, Mark and I saw thousands of people through their own journeys as we became spirit helpers in the medicine. I now know that my background as a coach stood me in such excellent stead, as I was able to hold space for people after their journeys as well as in them. I metaphorically held the hands of so many men and women, working through their trauma, healing and growth. It has been an honour. Some of the most important work I've ever done personally, and I've been working in self-development for women and female empowerment with thousands of women myself for the past 20 years.

For me, it brings everything I've been working on and learning in my life personally, together. I stood shoulder to shoulder with Mark, completely in love with the journey. Completely immersed in what we were doing.

My personal journey continues with Cacao & Ritual now, as I discover more about its significance in the lives of women and their families. My family and I have benefitted hugely from ayahuasca, and we are proud to be bringing our little girl Livvie up without biases about plant medicines. This little fledgling, our 'Shamamasita' (young shaman in the making), knows nothing else. For her, this sacred plant is a healer, a wise gift, an energy to respect.

Some of our guests say SHE brought US to the medicine, and I've thought many times that might be true. She blended with it and our guests so effortlessly and without resistance, totally accepting of other people, why they came for ayahuasca and what they struggle with in life. For her, the field of Mother Ayahuasca and her energy is magical. One day, if she feels the call, she will know if it's the right time for her and she'll go straight to Mother without fear.

For now, this book is about you. It's about your dalliance with the concept of ayahuasca, the concept of a Higher Power, the concept of what it could mean for you in your life. If you're drawn to this book, there will be a reason hidden somewhere in these pages. A word, a phrase, someone's account of their experience, something. Read it with an open mind, read it with love, read it with interest in Ren's personal story and his sharing it with you.

This book was Mother Ayahuasca's idea you could say, Ren the conduit, and so many others; little helpers in its fruition and now you, the reader, you're part of it too, and She is full of love and pure intent, without prejudice for every single human on Earth. Take her love, and Ren's, and see what you discover... A'ho!"

Lynette (Retreat host)

INTRODUCTION

This book was written because I was told to write it by 'Mother Ayahuasca' (as she is most commonly known) during my first ever experience of taking the psychedelic Amazonian plant medicine ayahuasca. Who or what 'Mother' is exactly, I can only speculate, and through speculation the obvious answers come to mind: Mother Nature, my own inner-voice, the voice of God? The truth is, I don't really know, but what I do know for certain is that something told me to stop writing my previous book *Anonymous God* and start writing this book.

It was suggested to me by Mother that this book would somehow help us change the world together, but we need evolution rather than revolution. I'm not sure how, but I hope this book helps you change in a way that is conducive to a more positive life. I presume you might be reading this book as a result of coincidence, serendipity, synchronicity, or a spiritual sign-post, or maybe you're questioning whether to drink ayahuasca yourself, as a way to assuage your suffering?

There's a theory many of us are beginning to realise that, as a species, we'll never free ourselves from suffering until we are all freed from suffering together. This echoes my life experience thus far; suffering the isolation and physical, mental, and emotional pain of active alcoholism for over 10 years, then recovering as part of a group (firstly, as a member of the Twelve Step fellowships, then additionally in my experience of drinking ayahuasca with a new-found 'tribe' of like-minded spiritual 'seekers').

As Gautama Buddha observed over 2500 years ago, life is full of suffering, and that suffering, in my opinion, is rooted in the pain of powerlessness, which we all have the capacity to feel. Most people deny that they are powerless, however, we are all powerless over other people, places, and things, and we don't like to admit that. Yet we know, and are comfortable, with being powerless over the weather for instance, or the fact that our physical body will one day die; that we can accept.

We have no problem admitting that we desire control, as being a 'control freak' seems to be more the norm these days. The kind of things you can control are: how you speak to yourself, who you follow, the boundaries you set, what you eat, your sleep routine, and when you ask for help. You can only control you, and the universal truth is that we have absolutely no control over anything external from ourselves – the rising and falling of life is un-controllable, and I would argue that it's fear that drives this need for control. We might want our children and our partners to behave in certain ways, we want the weather to be sunny at the weekends, and we want to know that we won't get stuck in traffic on our way to-and-from work. Most of us rarely 'go with the flow.'

Consider this, you are either living in fear or living in faith; they are reverse sides of the same coin. This is why it's suggested in Twelve Step fellowships to build a relationship with a Power that is greater than yourself, to help you handle your fear (one of your most natural and primal emotions) and learn to live free from suffering, with faith, rather than anxious or depressed – which are by-products of fear. Chinese philosopher Lao Tzu, best known for Taoism, said, "If you are depressed you are living in the past. If you are anxious you are living in the future. If you are at peace you are living in the present."

To my mind, faith is essentially the deeply held belief that we are all inextricably connected to each other and that this connection and sense of belonging is rooted in the Highest Power of all, which some people refer to as God. I'm pretty sure that, like me, you desire a wholehearted life – to feel that you are enough and that you belong, that you are loved and are capable of loving others. I'd say that we are all, therefore, searching for a Higher Power in some way – the power of connection and belonging, which led me to drink alcohol and take illicit drugs throughout my late teens and twenties – to connect with people, and to drink ayahuasca for the first time aged 37 – to reconnect with my soul.

On the day I was due to drink the infamous Amazonian plant medicine, an amazing coincidence occurred that affirmed to me that I was exactly where I was supposed to be at that time. On the 26th January 2018 in Mallorca, Spain, one of the retreat hosts asked me to hold the video camera and film a live-stream to pick the winner of a competition for a free weekend ayahuasca retreat. A fellow guest picked the first note out of a hat, which instructed to choose a letter for surnames at random. One of the hosts then chose the letter 'D,' which meant anyone on the Facebook group with 'D' in their surname was safe. Another note was picked from the hat, which instructed to choose a letter for forenames, and I chose the letter 'R,' which meant anyone on the Facebook group with 'R' in their forename was safe. This whittled the list down to 3 names. I was then asked to pick a number from 1 to 3 and

I chose 3. The name of the winner, to my astonishment, was Amber Dowler – a DJ I happen to have known since 2000 (we were both DJ's in the hard house scene for over ten years). Not only that, but the day before I flew out to Mallorca, I'd watched a video on Amber's Facebook page of her being interviewed ahead of an up-coming gig. I'd never been on Amber's Facebook page prior to that day but an invite from her had caught my attention. This astounding 'God-instance' settled my nerves and helped me realise, yet again, I was on the right path, and exactly where I was supposed to be in that moment. I sent a private message to Amber with a link to the video and she responded, "Probably the biggest synchronicity for me ever this!"

Synchronicity, I believe, is pertinent here, as you might have absolutely no idea why you were attracted to this book. Might I suggest that an underlying force – a Higher Power – is guiding you, making subtle suggestions, and this book is one of many suggested conduits to your continued spiritual awakening. By the time you've finished reading this book I hope you'll begin to question the nature of your pain and suffering, and understand that you can overcome it. I also hope you'll question the existence of a Higher Power in your own life, and realise that ayahuasca has meaningful messages for anyone who is a suitable health candidate, which might mean you.

I'm in no way claiming to be a mystic, and I'm not suggesting this book is in any way 'divinely inspired,' but given that every human being can be a mouthpiece for the divine – when we choose to be – communicating from our true-self (the soul) rather than our false-self (the ego), I believe this book was co-created in the sense that the words I've written are my interpretation of the information that came to me from 'beyond the veil,' so to speak, in the place of true-self – beyond the ego – in the psychedelic state, where Mother Ayahuasca held me safely.

Your heart-rate may well have elevated by now, your palms might feel slightly moist, you may well be thinking, how does this person know that I'm feeling both anxious and excited in this moment? I know because I've had that very same feeling when I was on the cusp of a great discovery; questioning the nature of reality and every aspect of my life, with my 'third-eye' steadily opening and the emotional pain becoming almost too much to bear. I know how it feels to be personally addressed by the words written on the pages of a book that somehow understood my suffering and offered me a solution to my pain. I also know how it feels to awaken to the splendour and magnificence of genuine human connection and belonging, to have glimpsed enlightenment and returned from what F. C. Happold termed the 'plenum-void' in his 1963 book *Mysticism: A Study and an Anthology* – safe in the knowledge that the salvation of mankind is right here, right now.

The fact you're reading this book might mean that you're beginning to understand that the answers to your questions and all the things you 'seek' are not to be found externally but inside you, in your heart. In order to be at peace with the world, you must first be at peace with yourself, and to truly enjoy life, you must first enjoy who you are, but this is not always easy.

All the great sages and mystics promised that once you learn how to master being peaceful, you'll be joyful and protected from everything that makes you feel anxious and depressed. And when you recognize yourself – who you are deep inside –

you'll never again feel lonely even when you're alone. You'll have tapped into a limitless Power Source that's available to you at all times, in all places. Some call it 'God,' and some call it enlightenment; having glimpsed it, thanks to my journey with Mother Ayahuasca, I now call it the 'Great Power of Love.'

0.0 SUFFERING

Suffering, such as distress, loss and grief, confusion, guilt, shame, and trauma (of which we very rarely speak about and don't know what to do with the feelings), is a big part of life for everyone, and we are all vulnerable to it, so it should bring us closer together, but it often isolates us. Aversion to suffering is one of the greatest diminishers of life experience; if you're always turning away from your difficulties, you'll never get very far. The fact of the matter is, you can't close your heart down to suffering or you'll be forever at the mercy of it.

Paradoxically, suffering is considered 'Grace' (a divinely given blessing) from the perspective of the spiritually enlightened, as it's often a catalyst for spiritual awakening. Grace is something that a wise individual can attribute to their suffering and use it to their own advantage; to evolve. Suffering involves bearing the unbearable yet I've come to believe that who you think you are (your ego) can't bear it, but what you really are (a soul) can.

As a recovering alcoholic and member of Twelve Step fellowships since 2010, and working in the 'substance misuse' field since 2013, I encounter human suffering in the form of substance and behavioural addictions on a daily basis, and I find myself perfectly placed in a position of privilege where I'm able to comprehend viable solutions to the addiction problem, and the problem of human suffering in general. I consider my alcoholism to be Grace, as my suffering led to my sobriety, then to my spiritual awakening, which led to me becoming more compassionate and loving. My suffering evolved me.

In 2016 I wrote my first book *Addiction Prevention: Twelve Steps To Spiritual Awakening*, which outlines a proposal to introduce Twelve Step classes into the education system, as a means of addiction prevention and to help young people overcome mental health issues. One of the most important observations I've made is that there's a distinct absence of belonging, meaning, and purpose, in the life of the 'chronic addict' – an individual who's typically suffered with the disease of addiction (including alcoholism) for a long period of time. I believe the introduction of the Twelve Step Program into primary school education for instance, would help to prevent the onset of mental illnesses that people attempt to medicate with addictive substances and damaging behaviours later in life. It would also help young people to find purpose, meaning, and belonging, as they'd be oriented toward a life of spiritual values (love and service) rather than materialistic values, such as the pursuit of happiness through money, power, and prestige.

From a young age I've contemplated the meaning of my existence and I've been fascinated by the deeper mysteries of life: Who am I? Why am I here? What is my purpose? What is God? I'm intrigued by the notion of 'higher states of consciousness,' and the concept of a 'Higher Power.' My dad's mother was a Roman Catholic and my mom's mother was a Protestant Christian, and both grandmothers took me with them to church a few times before my dad's mom died when I was twelve. After that, I rarely stepped foot in churches, unless on school trips or visiting historical sites on vacations.

Neither of my parents are religious, although my dad gained strength from his Catholic upbringing when he got sober in Alcoholics Anonymous. "God grant me the serenity to accept the things I cannot change, the courage to change the things I can, and the wisdom to know the difference. Thy will, not mine, be done," read the plaque next to his bed. I thought he'd turned religious but I didn't care, so long as he didn't force his religion on me, which, thankfully, he never did.

Ironically, I took my first alcoholic drink the same year my dad stopped drinking but I opted not to continue, as I was a keen sportsman, and I knew what had become of famous alcoholic athletes such as Manchester United legend George Best and England legend Paul Gascoigne. I promised myself I'd never end up an alcoholic, but in hindsight, I had no choice in the matter because I have a physical intolerance to alcohol, which I was either born with or developed over time. With schoolmates, I became known for not drinking or smoking (which was uncommon) until my 16th birthday when I tried cannabis for the first time with my best friend David – who was already a keen smoker. It made me feel paranoid, so I rarely smoked 'weed' after that, unless I was too 'high' on other drugs and wanted to 'come down.'

Aged 17, I drank some alcoholic beverages at a soccer awards ceremony – where I gained accolades for my accomplished performances. This time the alcohol had a profound effect on me. I thought I was drinking to be sociable but in retrospect, it was because I was no longer resilient enough to resist peer group pressure, and I didn't have the courage to rebel against the status quo anymore, so instead I copied my friends. There was a real sense of ease and comfort that came with those drinks – an inner warmth as though my pilot light had been switched on, like I was lit up from the inside. I instantly became funnier, better looking, more confident, and more intelligent – or so I thought! From that point on, my obsession for sport was replaced by an obsession for alcohol, music, drugs and sex – usually in that order!

No-one, and nothing in particular, is to blame for my alcoholism. My mom and dad are very good people, who did a wonderful job of raising me with the tools they had at their disposal. Materially, I've never wanted for anything, and I've always felt loved. When I was younger, however, my dad was often away with work and because he drank alcohol every day, I assume that when he was home, he was emotionally unavailable – like I became when I got drunk – but I can't actually remember much about that time. Mom did her best to control me but I was a defiant child, so my dad had to discipline me quite often. It's written in the book *Alcoholics Anonymous*, "As psychiatrists have often observed, defiance is the outstanding characteristic of many an alcoholic."

I had the 'spiritual malady' (restlessness, irritability, discontentment) long before I picked up an alcoholic drink. I unwittingly medicated myself with sugar, TV, and an obsession with music. My gran was horrified once when she saw how badly I behaved at home, as I acted like an angel when I was with her and my granddad. I was disobedient with some teachers at school and regularly sent out of class for 'acting the fool.' I also got into fights with other kids quite frequently. I was full of rage.

There was unequivocally no lack of love in my family but looking back, I feel that I didn't get my needs met in certain areas because we didn't talk about our feelings. Throughout my teens, my dad and I argued a lot. We both had quick tempers and there was a lot of unresolved anger from both sides, so we rarely settled disputes peacefully. I resented his authority and rebelled at practically every opportunity. When I left home for university it felt like the 'shackles' were off and I hastily set off down the road to freedom, but I took an accidental wrong turn down a path to the destination marked 'self-destruction.'

Blackouts, whereby my mind went home and I stayed out to play, morning vomiting, and plenty of guilt and shame following drunken shenanigans became a regular occurrence. I perceived that I was getting so much enjoyment at the loss of my inhibitions that I was to drink alcoholically for the next ten years. In retrospect, alcohol never made me happy, it merely rendered me oblivious to my feelings, and my surroundings, and gave me a false sense of pleasure.

Aged 18, I moved from my home city of Manchester to Leeds to further my education at university. There, I 'partied' almost every night, and I didn't learn much else other than how to drink and take drugs. I have no desire to glamorise my story, and there are many 'drink-a-logs' and 'drug-a-logs' out there already; I simply drank every day and I used drugs often. Practically everybody I hung-out with during my time at university drank alcohol and used drugs like I did, but as we grew older, they either calmed down, stopped altogether, died in various ways, or like me – they carried on.

I DJ'd and danced for over 10 years in the underground hard-house music scene, which was insanely (and in hindsight tragically) fun when I was in my early twenties. My perception of 'rave culture' and dance-club environments changed, however, after I got sober. I became painfully aware that I was in fact 'spinning tunes' to large groups of emotionally and mentally unwell people who venerated the DJ like a demigod inside elaborately decorated mental asylums. The vast majority of 'clubbers' were escaping reality by using copious amounts of alcohol and drugs while ritualistically swaying, dancing, and singing – like a modern-day ecclesiastical congregation – to the hypnotic rhythm of electronically synthesised tribal drum beats. Hence, why, one night in 2012, during the biggest gig of my DJ career, I looked out across the sea of clubbers on the dance-floor and realised that, ethically, DJing was no longer for me and crucially, I was no longer interested in chasing fame, which can be an addiction in itself. I walked away from the drug-fuelled 'clubbing' scene and I've never looked back.

In my first year at university I was introduced to the drug ecstasy. One can only describe the effects of ecstasy as a synthesised spiritual experience. As I transcended waking consciousness, it dissolved the boundary of my ego and all my insecurities melted away. The love I felt for everyone I encountered that first night on ecstasy was all encompassing and so powerful that the next day I decided I would take 'pills' as often as I could. What goes up, however, must come down, and three years later, by the age of twenty-one, having consumed ten 'E's' on New Year's Day and ten 'E's' the night before, I realised the ecstasy had stopped working. I was no longer experiencing the same intensity of loved-up 'high,' and when I wasn't taking ecstasy, I felt utterly miserable. By my mid-twenties, I was 'spiritually bankrupt,' and so far-removed from my emotions that I felt empty. My mental health was suffering as I became more and more depressed – so much so that my friends intervened and told me all the reasons why I needed to stop. Little did they know, I replaced ecstasy for cocaine and for the next five years I drank alcohol most nights and used cocaine regularly to help me drink more alcohol.

The less drugs I used, the more my drinking escalated and by 2009, at the age of twenty-eight, I needed alcohol every night and I rarely went out at after work because I was in-doors, on my own, drinking myself into oblivion. My drinking went on like this for about a year before my girlfriend Sally suggested we leave Leeds and go to live in Australia for a while – to get away from my problems. Of course, you take your problems with you wherever you go, as your problems are all in your mind.

0.1 THE PALACE OF WISDOM

"The road of excess leads to the palace of wisdom," according to English poet William Blake. Eventually, I woke up from my nightmare and set off down the path toward freedom from my addictions. On the morning of September 7th 2009, I awoke from (what I hope to be) my final alcoholic blackout and I knew the game was over. After over-hearing Sally telling her sister she would leave me if I didn't change my behaviour, I got down on my knees and I prayed to a God I didn't even believe existed, asking Him to help me, as I couldn't continue doing what I was doing to myself and the people I loved anymore. I was sick and tired of being sick and tired.

When I stood up from that prayer, something inside my chest shifted; it was like a blockage around my heart had been dislodged and simultaneously the war in my mind (shall I drink today or not?) was over. I'd surrendered to the fact I can't drink safely. I felt total serenity – a revelation that can't be accurately reported; I believe Catholics refer to it as being 'reborn,' or 'Born Again.'

That night I had the best sleep of my life to date. Days later, I realised the mental obsession for alcohol had been completely removed from my mind. I was surrounded by alcohol in Thailand, and in Australia, but I had no desire to drink. For the following nine months I didn't use any mind-altering substances until one day, I randomly found a bag of cannabis in the caravan park where Sally and I lived and worked, rolled a 'joint,' and smoked it on the beach. I smoked the cannabis because, after six months of mental clarity – feeling great physically and wondering why I ever drank or used drugs in the first place, my mind descended into extremely resentful, homicidal, and suicidal thoughts; it was like a washing machine, sloshing and spinning a poisonous cocktail of toxicity round and round. I constantly felt anxious and stressed, and I wanted out. I thought the cannabis would help but it didn't; it made me feel physically sick, increased my anxiety, and I felt extremely paranoid. I wrote in my journal that evening, 'I will never use drugs or drink alcohol ever again.'

I rang my dad the next day who suggested I try a Twelve Step meeting but I politely declined. Secretly, in my opinion, Twelve Step fellowships were religious groups and my dad was weak to need those people. I thought I could do it on my own. I was too prideful to drink alcohol but ironically too full of pride, and my own self-importance, to ask for help.

Three months later, in London, following a year in Australia, I was back down on my knees begging God for help. I broke down. I couldn't take it anymore. There was a rage inside me that I was struggling to tame and I felt like I should drink or kill myself; I didn't consciously contemplate the necessary steps to suicide but my thoughts and feelings were unbearable. I rang my dad again and told him I was going to try a Twelve Step meeting.

When I arrived at the church in North London, I was greeted by happy, smiley people, laughing and joking; they were very welcoming. It seemed a bit suspect. I was waiting for 'the catch.' I sat at the back of the meeting and listened, as they had suggested, for the similarities in people's stories and not the differences. There were many, especially when people spoke about their feelings such as fear, anger, guilt, shame, remorse, and sadness. At last I knew what was wrong with me!

I'd found my tribe. After the meeting had finished, it seemed like I floated home, declaring to Sally that I was an alcoholic and I would never drink again! It was a huge weight off my shoulders – a complete unburdening.

In my early days of recovery, people suggested that I don't make any major decisions in my first year, as it was likely I'd make impulsive choices to attempt to make myself feel better now that I no longer had my perceived 'crutch' alcohol. I didn't listen and instead, I found myself a new job, and married my fiancé Sally within two months.

Needless to say, the job and my marriage didn't last. I was attempting to fix my outside before fixing my inside. I had a moment of serenity on my wedding day, similar to that which I experienced the morning after my last drink, but retrospectively, deep down, I knew the relationship wasn't quite 'right' because my discreet inner-voice had been telling me so for a few years. In truth, I felt guilty and ashamed that I couldn't give Sally the love she deserved but I was too scared to leave the person who was holding me together, who had loved me unconditionally, and who I'd loved dearly for many years. I will always be shamefaced and remorseful about this, and I feel that the best way of making amends is to leave her alone and pray for her continued happiness in life.

As I began to change due to my newfound sobriety, the wheels of our relationship slowly started to come off. Couples either grow together or they grow apart, and in our case, sadly, we grew apart – mainly due to my inability to form a true, loving partnership. Our nine-year relationship ended in separation, and the divorce was finalised two years later in 2012. The break-up was one of the worst periods of my life thus far. It upset me so much to see my wife and best friend distressed because of me, and I was so full of fear about the future that I almost drank on several occasions. I instead self-medicated, first with food, then sex with other women. It wasn't until my sponsor suggested that I "up my game" in terms of working my program – specifically praying and meditating, writing gratitude lists, taking inventory, and being of service to others – that things got better.

I left London briefly in 2014 and spent two months in Gran Canaria with my Italian friends Massi, Helli, and their son Lorenzo, where I concluded that I wanted to embark on a career as a counselling psychologist. I emailed my parents to tell them I'd decided to move back to London to study. They were initially concerned about how I'd pay for this education but randomly my mom came across an advertisement for an 'Apprentice Drug and Alcohol Counsellor' with a London-based charity, which included training for a Level 3 Counselling diploma. The only criteria were applicants had to be at least three years abstinent from drugs and alcohol, and I was four years in recovery at the time, so I sent my application from Gran Canaria, got offered an interview, moved back to East London, passed the three-interview-process, and began working for the charity in a West London prison in February 2015.

I completed my one-year apprenticeship at the prison then transferred to a South West London prison for a permanent counsellor position with the charity – where I worked until 2017. During those two years I went to a minimum of four Twelve Step meetings per week and I saw three counsellors bi-weekly for roughly six months each, which helped me to stabilise my life and forgive myself for the mistakes of my past.

I've since acquired a sanguine view of life and changed everything to serve my life purpose, which I believe is to help people. I've experienced lots of change and I've had to make some tough choices, and ride some rough waves, but the sea is slowly beginning to settle down for me and I'm experiencing more and more serenity. Every now and then the waves get choppy but I know that I'm safe in my recovery lifeboat providing I stay in the middle of the boat.

0.2 UNIVERSAL ADDICTION

My inherent belief is that addiction is universal. We're all addicted to something, and I think the solution to the addiction problem is faith in a Higher Power (of your own understanding). The medical profession declared back in the 1930's that they don't have a solution to the addiction problem, and over 80 years later they still don't have a medical solution. There's no pharmaceutical remedy for alcoholism, and pharmaceutical medications for heroin addiction, or any other substance for that matter, are analogous to using a small Band-Aid to cover a gaping wound. Medications simply don't address the addict's underlying issues. They are treatment not therapy, and in most cases the addict becomes reliant on the medication (such as Physeptone or Buprenorphine as a replacement for heroin), which is essentially cross-addiction. The person, therefore, never recovers from addiction to substances. 'Big Pharma,' however, is fast beginning to realise the healing power of plant medicines, which will hopefully limit the utilisation of expansive therapies that have marginal benefits, and the reliance on synthesised medications.

The first aim of my second book *Anonymous God*, written in 2018, was to show that evidence of a Higher Power is all around us all the time – in the form of coincidence, serendipity, synchronicity and spiritual sign-posts, which might awaken people to the wonderment of their current human journey and help them discover meaning in their lives that may otherwise have remained hidden. The second aim was to demonstrate that psychedelic plant medicines are a viable tool for healing from trauma, and that connection with a Higher Power undeniably helps with human suffering.

The aim of this book is to explain how everyone can overcome their pain and suffering by connecting with a Higher Power through the use of psychedelic plant medicines such as ayahuasca – especially those who are spiritually 'blocked.' I'm convinced that if an alcoholic/addict has a massive, undeniable spiritual experience, like I had with ayahuasca, they would then be more open to the concept of a Higher Power that could restore them to sanity from the insanity of addiction. Drinking ayahuasca, therefore, was partly a research experiment to determine whether the medicine could be helpful in the treatment of addiction, and partly to help me with my own suffering. The following pages are my record of that experience.

0.3 THERE IS AN ANSWER

I'm a bit of a loner and a deep thinker. I'm also a dreamer. I have a big heart and I'm very passionate about life. I see there are lots of things wrong with our society and for some reason I've never felt like I fit in anywhere. I'm socially awkward. I'm too weird for the 'normal' people and too normal for the weird people. I often feel like an outsider and I always have, but I'm comfortable with that now. Self-discovery throughout my sobriety has changed everything, including my relationships with all the people in my life. When I got sober and found my authentic self, those who loved my mask were disappointed and exited my life. I felt lonely for a while, but I didn't stay lonely. It was quite painful severing old connections but it wasn't a tragedy, as it was an opportunity to find other people who understand the importance of being authentic and honest. I'm now a small but integral part of the greatest spiritual movement of our time in Twelve Step fellowships. I've found people who want to connect deeply, like I always wanted to in my addiction, as opposed to 'small-talk' and bullshit mind-games. I found my tribe and re-discovered myself, and now I have real intimacy with my fellows, and with my family and friends.

I'm an idealist and an optimist but I spent much of my early years riddled with insecurity and self-doubt, and people-pleasing habits, which made me pessimistic, anxious, and depressed. My spiritual journey began when my comfortable, middle-class life, was derailed by the unexpected darkness of alcoholism. My trusted methods of coping (alcohol and drugs) stopped working, and I was desperately unhappy. I was convinced back then, in my depression, that I'd never experience joy again, but ultimately, my misery and despair set me off on a quest for something more; for truth, wisdom, and love. Once the adventure began, there was no stopping this dreamer, and when I found ever more dreamers, I realised that we *can* change the world for the better, *together*.

I'm often governed by my inner child, who acts in a spontaneous way. As time passes, I'm getting better at expressing my emotions and I like to be able to share my sense of excitement and laughter, and play the fool with others, who are on the same level. I can be serious but I generally don't like to take myself too seriously, and I'm happy to go with the flow and let most things take their course. 'C'est la vie' is tattoo'd on my arm, which sums me up, as I accept life on life's terms. Although I really get into the things I do, I also flit from one thing to the next fairly regularly, and I often act on impulse – following my needs and wants in the moment – to capitalise on my enthusiasm and momentum. My inner child is like a firecracker, going off this way and that, always wanting to be in on any adventure going. If I let my inner child express itself within a stable and nurturing environment – like at home with my girlfriend Adele and her two children, and give it constructive guidance, then it's very useful to me. On the other hand, if I let my inner child simply do its own thing, I risk becoming chaotic and unmanageable (as I was for many years in active alcoholism), and ending up as a boy who never grew up!

I was finally ready to grow up and take responsibility for my life when I made the decision to take ayahuasca. I was first introduced to the concept of 'ayahuasca treatment' by a friend in 2014. Prior to any investigation, my initial reaction was contempt, "Are you crazy mate? You can't do that, it would be a relapse!"

Having been in recovery for over four years at the time, I didn't believe there were any viable treatment alternatives for addiction. However, the more I've learned since then, from my previous vocation as a Drug and Alcohol Counsellor in UK prisons, plus lots of personal research about alternative treatments for mental health issues and addiction, the more the healing properties of ayahuasca (and other traditional medicines, such as Iboga and San Pedro) have seemed practical and become more appealing.

The scientific evidence on ayahuasca treatment is limited but retreat centres, such as Rythmia in Costa Rica, have been approved by the U.S. Food and Drug Administration (FDA), as ayahuasca is known to activate repressed memories and help people work through memories of traumatic events, which is why neuroscientists are beginning to study ayahuasca as a treatment for depression and PTSD.

In 2016 I felt a calling from deep within to 'journey' with ayahuasca. Initially I ignored this calling until 2017 when it became clear to me that it was something I needed to do, as I felt I couldn't keep writing about the subject without experiencing it for myself.

Prior to making the decision, I'd traumatically and regrettably ended my relationship with my girlfriend Adele while we were on holiday. We'd been through a lengthy period of outer turmoil and inner purging and I'd lost faith in us, which led to me leaving. The ecstasy from the initial 'falling in love' period had worn off, our individual egos had flared up, and suddenly, we had major differences in opinion on a regular basis. Old core wounds were emerging out of the gloom and we were continuously mirroring each-others shadow-selves, and riling up each-others insecurities. Communication between us had become fragmented; this was initially infuriating, then devastating, and very painful.

The night Adele and I arrived back home following a dreadfully upsetting last two days, and a miserable flight home, I said goodbye to Adele's mom (who was at our house looking after the kids) the only way I knew how, which was detached and emotionless, and the next morning I packed my belongings and moved out. I felt that Adele had betrayed me, and I'd betrayed her.

I decided to use my time alone as a period of retreat, and do all the things I'd always wanted to do for myself. As a conscious explorer exploring consciousness, drinking ayahuasca was top of my 'bucket list,' as I hoped it would help me figure out what to do next, and if there was any hope of Adele and I getting back together.

Sometimes all we need in order to change is a little wisdom, spoken to us wIth gentleness and a pure heart. 'Mother Ayahuasca' spoke to me gently and enlightened me with her wisdom, and I returned from Mallorca with a message for anyone who cared to listen, and lessons that could be applied by anyone who cared to learn.

My experience was beautiful and profound. I went beyond the confines of my 'ego' and I understood what it meant to be interconnected with all sentient beings, and connected to the Élan Vital (the universal life-force, as proposed by French philosopher Henri Bergson in his 1907 book *Creative Evolution*). I saw, and truly understood, that there's an incredible Power inside all of us – a Life Force that's waiting to break free, so we can reach our full potential. I also saw that the time has come for my potential to be realised.

Something has been blocking me from reaching my true potential; a fog has been pursuing me since childhood, bringing with it one problem after another, especially as far as money and relationships are concerned. This fog I now recognise to be my ego, which has always prevented me from enjoying my potential success. No more.

We all receive, at birth, the potential for incredible things, which is in strong contrast to the many difficulties we experience in later life – plus elements of bad luck that we all encounter. We must, therefore, develop faith in ourselves, our ideas, and our initiatives. We must also develop the ability to hold our head high and persevere when things go wrong, then we'll be able to move forward in life – even in the most delicate or hazardous of times, which is something I've struggled with at various times in my life. No more.

As things currently stand, I take each day as it comes, without really knowing what will happen tomorrow. 'Keep it in the day' is my motto. In the past, any time I had a plan with a goal, I always achieved it, but sometimes – maybe due to a lack of self-confidence – I made bad decisions, which had serious consequences; then I'd get stuck in a cycle of guilt and regret. No more.

Following my experience with ayahuasca, I've now realised that I have everything I need *within me* to succeed and accomplish my life goals. It's possible that unfortunate circumstances in my past affected me, forcing me to make bad decisions, but I'll no longer dwell on the past, nor worry about what the future holds. The time is Now.

On the day I arrived home from my ayahuasca experience, I received an email from *The Sacred Science* website. It contained a powerful, Native American, Lakota tribe prayer, which compounded the magnificence of my mysterious, enlightening experience with ayahuasca. I believe it was a message from the universe for me and it re-focused my awareness on the lessons that 'Mother Ayahuasca' had taught me – that there is an answer to all my, and the world's, problems:

"Great Mystery,
Teach me how to trust my heart, my mind, my intuition,
my inner knowing, the senses of my body,
the blessings of my spirit.
Teach me to trust these things so that I may enter my sacred space and love beyond my fear, and thus walk in balance with the passing of each glorious sun."

1.0 PREPARATION

Flotation is widely advertised as a form of alternative medicine, with claims that it has beneficial health effects on conditions including muscle tension, chronic pain, hypertension, and rheumatoid arthritis. A float tank is a lightless, soundproof tank filled with salt water at skin temperature in which one floats. They were first used in 1954 to test the effects of sensory deprivation. Comedian and podcast host Joe Rogan has popularised their use, as he regularly discusses his extensive sensory-deprivation tank experience on his podcast *The Joe Rogan Experience*. My first 'float' evoked mild hallucinations. Just for fun, I asked out loud, "God what should I do next?" and a voice in from the darkness clearly replied, "Be joyful!"

Following my float, I began preparation for my ayahuasca retreat, which meant a vegan diet for one week prior to the ceremony – avoiding not only meat but alcohol (easy because I don't drink), caffeine, fermented foods, chocolate (difficult!), dairy products, avocados, bananas, mushrooms, heavy sugars, salts and spices, and abstaining from all sexual activity for three days leading up to the ceremony – to allow my base sexual energy to accumulate and help facilitate personal transformation. I'd also confirmed to the team at the ayahuasca retreat in Mallorca that I wasn't taking any prescribed medication, or illicit drugs, and I'd also disclosed my previous state of health.

It was suggested by one of the retreat hosts that I bring an intention to the ceremony, which is an intended outcome, but to hold my intention in my mind with nurturing love rather than gripping it with anxious fear that it might not happen. It was also suggested that I be light and joyful with my intention (which I felt was synchronistic following my float experience) and during the ceremony to simply relax, trust that 'Mother Ayahuasca' knows best and has my best interests at heart, breathe, and surrender. Everybody's experience is unique I'd read, so it's best to let go of any expectations and be accepting of whatever comes up, and be free and flowing with ayahuasca's magic.

In the past few decades ayahuasca has gained increasing interest from Western spiritual 'seekers.' Academic researchers in the field of psychotherapy, and 'Psychonauts' (people who practice responsible and conscious use of mind-altering substances), use ayahuasca to confront themselves and the infinity of the universe, and to experience the feeling of ecstasy resulting from facing and overcoming their deepest fears.

Ayahuasca is capable of inducing altered states of consciousness, usually lasting from 4 to 8 hours after ingestion – ranging from mildly stimulating to extremely visionary. It's used primarily as a medicine, and as a spiritual means of communication, typically in a ceremonial environment under the guidance of one or more experienced shaman. The main ingredient of the brew is the Banisteriopsis caapi vine (B.caapi), which is a monoamine oxidase inhibitor (MAOI) allowing for ingestion, and like the brew itself is also called ayahuasca (translating to 'vine of the soul'). The secondary ingredient is either Psychotria viridis (chacruna) or Diplopterys cabrerana leaves (also known as chaliponga and chacropanga) that contain a relatively high amount of the psychedelic substance N, N-Dimethyltryptamine (DMT). This neurotransmitter is found in the brain, blood, lungs, and other parts of the human body. There is strong evidence pointing towards the pineal gland ('the third-eye' in esoteric traditions), located in the centre of the brain, as the main factory of DMT in humans but this has not yet been proven. DMT can also be found in every mammal on Earth, and in a variety of plants. Many people have suggested it's there for a reason and is meant to be accessed.

Part of the ayahuasca process is the purge, known as 'la purga' (most commonly experienced as vomiting and diarrhoea but also shaking, yawning, laughing, or crying), which is part of the process of purifying the body and mind. Mother Ayahuasca may also take you through vivid emotional experiences and visions. Psychonauts usually feel totally refreshed and 'reborn' after a strong experience. There are also many fascinating anecdotal reports about people who've healed themselves from comprehensive problems, such as addiction or depression. As a recovering alcoholic working in the 'substance misuse' field, the notion of healing alcoholism and addiction greatly interests me, as there's currently no known pharmaceutical cure. Total abstinence is the only solution when all attempts at moderation fail.

Ayahuasca is not said to be a miracle cure in the sense that you drink the brew and all of your troubles vanish within a couple of hours. It is, however, a miracle cure in the sense that it brings unconscious and seemingly other-worldly processes to the surface, which enables the drinker to work through them while the effects last, then take the lessons away with them into their everyday living – known as 'integration.' Ayahuasca enables the brain to temporarily override old patterns and create new connections; old fears may no longer have the same effect because the memories are re-evaluated during the 'trip,' although the user may not be aware of this process at all. Ayahuasca takes the 'default mode network' in the brain, which is a defence system that regulates information coming in from outside sources and up from within, offline. Once the default mode network is switched off, the information can flow freely, which opens up the doors of perception – often resulting in revelatory visions.

Ayahuasca drinkers also often develop new perspectives on their past experiences and deeply rooted patterns of behaviour. This is why quitting from bad habits can be 'easier' following an ayahuasca experience (so long as they integrate properly and use their experiences wisely). Freedom from trauma, depression, and many other ailments, is entirely possible – the list of reported benefits is endless.

The short-term effects of ayahuasca differ from one individual to another but most people feel that they heal from past trauma and painful psychological experiences during ayahuasca sessions. There's also very limited data about the long-term adverse psychological effects of ayahuasca, however, a number of studies have revealed that ayahuasca doesn't have any at all. Director General at Clínica Galatea in Barcelona, Spain, Dr. Josep Fabregas, co-author of the 2010 study of the long-term effects of ayahuasca, also concluded that ayahuasca is not addictive; on the contrary, ayahuasca treatment combats addiction because it helps patients reconcile their past trauma.

I believe the answer to the addiction problem might be using traditional plant medicines, such as ayahuasca to induce a spiritual awakening, followed by intensive Twelve Step therapy, which in my opinion is the most comprehensive spiritual program known to man – and proven to be affective in the treatment of the underlying emotional and mental health issues that people attempt to medicate with addictive substances and obsessive-compulsive behaviours.

In early life, powerful or traumatic events create an imprint (or pattern) on the brain. This pattern is like a shortcut, activated every time we face a similar situation. For example, if we were once attacked by a dog, our brain might harbour a set of pathways that associate that dog with all dogs, making us fear dogs in general; we might even react adversely to a distant bark. Repeated events cause these neural patterns to reinforce their connections, binding them with protein and building them up like scar tissue. Ayahuasca hyper-activates the entire brain region where we store and process emotional memory (the highly evolved neo-cortex), often uncovering long-forgotten memories. This hyper-activation of areas in the brain, such as the amygdala, which acts as a storehouse for early emotional memories (specifically the most traumatic or significant ones), enables the conscious part of the brain to temporarily override previously entrenched patterns, allowing new connections to be made. Suffering, therefore, ceases to be suffering as we form a clear and precise picture of it, and dogs may no longer be feared, as these new connections are created and memories are re-evaluated.

In research studies, ayahuasca users typically describe having a new perspective on past experiences and deeply rooted patterns of behaviour, as ayahuasca also activates the insula, which is believed to create a bridge between our emotional impulses and our decision-making capacities.

Ayahuasca arguably offers many positive impacts for the body, mind, and soul. It seems that the medicine very efficiently helps in the treatment of emotional pain, physical ailments, and emotional and mental illnesses – including addictions, and various fears including the fear of mortality.

People with a less-defined diagnoses, but a hunger for something they feel is 'missing,' say that ayahuasca overwhelmingly offers compassion, love, joy, empathy, connectedness, and spiritual 'oneness.' When used in conjunction with a healthy lifestyle and spiritual practices such as yoga, prayer, and meditation, ayahuasca can have a strong and positive impact on the emotional and cognitive processes of an individual, and can facilitate spiritual awakening, understanding, healing, and the enhancement of universal wisdom.

The effects and results may vary from person to person, and one must be willing to have a very long and powerful internal experience, but undoubtedly the medicine can change a person's life and transform them into a whole new individual – with a renewed spirit and vigour.

Ayahuasca, therefore, can be a life-changing emotional catharsis, and can ultimately facilitate the death of all the negativity that you think you are; however, it only reveals what is already inside one's own heart and mind. Following this 'Little Death' (as it's known in the Amazon) comes the resurrection; a new, fresh, original being, which many 'seekers' were not even aware was hidden within. Following this 'rebirth,' it's difficult not to want to work hard and continue to change, but it can also be easy to get stuck back in the old habitual patterns we were attempting to out-grow in the first place, hence the need for focused and intentional integration post ceremony.

1.1 A WALK IN THE WOODS

I arrived in Mallorca having read *What is Zen?* by Alan Watts from cover to cover on the plane journey, so I was feeling pretty 'zen' and my mind was prepared for what was about to happen – as prepared as it could be going into my first ayahuasca experience.

I sat in Palma airport meditating for half an hour, waiting for one of the retreat hosts to pick me up. When Mark arrived, we hugged like long lost brothers – even though we'd never met – and he drove us to the retreat centre.

By the time we arrived it was gone midnight. Mark showed me around the place, as best he could in the dark – pointing out the bathroom, lounge, and outdoor seating area, where two of the guests stood chatting. We walked the fifty-yard path, lit with dim-yellow lanterns, to the large wooden circular Mongolian yurt – where the ceremonies take place. Eight people lay sleeping on mattresses under blankets in sleeping bags, and an empty mattress awaited me. Mark assured me, even though it might seem a bit weird, that all was good, and I should, "hit the sack."
I didn't feel weird at all.

Mark wondered off to the house as I made my way to the bathroom. I washed my face and brushed my teeth, then I headed back to the yurt and settled down in my sleeping bag for a broken night's sleep. People were in-and-out of the yurt all night, and there were a few snorers. I was, however, lovely and warm under my thick green fleece blanket, stationed near the log fire, and my sense of adventure kept me from feeling anything other than positively intrigued and excited.

The next morning, I showered, then relaxed in the lounge, eating a breakfast of porridge and fruit, drinking green tea, and getting to know my fellow 'seekers.' At that point I was the only person in the group who hadn't taken the medicine before – most people had 'drank' multiple times.

No-one spoke in any great detail of their previous experiences, they all just assured me I'd be fine and that each person's experience is often very different from the next person. We spoke about our 'intentions.' I shared that my intentions were: to figure out if Adele and I were meant to be together (as we had recently started communicating again following two months of no contact after our break-up); to drop selfishness; to become more open and honest in my relationships; and to meet God.

I was assured by Leanne – a fiery, intelligent Scotswoman with dark brown hair and kind, knowing, blue eyes – that 'Mother Ayahuasca' sees where I've been and where I'm going on my journey, and that She would show me exactly what I needed to see. Nervous excitement was building.

After we ate lunch in the lounge, a guy called Luke arrived and we instantly connected. We both hail from Manchester, and he reminded me of my cousin due to his dark hair, boyish good looks, and wicked sense of humour. Shortly after our initial introduction, Luke, Leanne, a jolly Slovenian woman named Natasha, and I, decided to go for a long walk in the surrounding countryside, as there were no other plans ahead of the ceremony that night, the sun was shining gloriously, and it would be a while until the rest of the 'seekers' arrived.

We walked for around three hours through lush green fields, sparse forests, and winding tarmac lanes, in a huge circle and back to base, during which time we had lots of deep and meaningful conversations about our life situations, the universe, synchronicity, and why we believed we had been called to 'journey' with ayahuasca.

I explained to Luke that I was currently writing a book entitled *Anonymous God* – about coincidence, serendipity, synchronicity, and spiritual signposts – and that the penultimate chapter, which addressed the use of psychedelic drugs, would be concluded with my ayahuasca experience. I explained how drinking the brew for research purposes would very likely be considered a 'relapse' by my fellows in Twelve Step recovery, which is the reason I'd only told two fellow recovering alcoholics – who didn't necessarily agree with what I was doing, but they didn't pass judgement either. My friends outside of recovery circles were eager to know what the experience was like but they were fearful of drinking ayahuasca themselves for many reasons, including not being ready to face their own 'demons.'

Having been through the psychotherapeutic Twelve Step process multiple times since 2010, and having years of psychotherapy with counsellors, I felt that I'd already faced most of my demons, and I was ready to face any demons that might arise during the ceremony, which, in actuality, turned out not to be the case, as I wasn't ready to face the 'addiction demon.'

We arrived back at base just as more seekers were turning up and making themselves comfortable. Moments after the cherry sun had disappeared behind the dark green, forest-clad horizon, Amy – a tall, slim Londoner with long blonde hair, blue eyes, and a gold nose ring – sat down next to me and introduced herself. I was still coughing and spluttering and finding it difficult to concentrate on her conversation, as moments earlier, Luke and I had been introduced to rapé (a rare sacred shamanic snuff medicine, which is pronounced 'ha-peh' in English) by trainee shaman Austin; a tall, slim, dark haired Bristolian with a goatee beard and calm disposition.

Austin had applied the rapé by using a pipe made from bamboo, which he blew up each of my nostrils – left then right. Ahead of the ceremony, I was told this would prepare me by opening up all my chakras, grounding me, releasing any physical, emotional, mental, or spiritual sickness, opening up my 'third-eye' by de-calcifying the pineal gland, clearing any mental confusion, releasing any negative thoughts, removing any 'entities,' connecting me to my divine breath, and elevating my connection with Source. I wasn't convinced any of that happened at the time, as I felt fine beforehand, but I vomited after rapé and once my pounding headache had subsided, my head did feel 'cleansed,' and I also felt composed and alert.

Neither Amy, Luke, nor I, had experienced ayahuasca before, so we related as novices, chatting about meditation, yoga, and spirituality, as the nervous excitement ahead of the ceremony continued to build.

1.2 AMY'S STORY (PART 1)

"The first time I attempted to go to an 'ayahuasca retreat' I ended up missing my flight through a series of very unfortunate events including taking a wrong turn, getting stuck behind a pile of lorries in a petrol station, and finding myself at the wrong gate on the opposite side of the airport – for whatever reason, it wasn't my time.

So, the second time around – when on my way to the airport I missed my turning AGAIN, I began to doubt that ayahuasca was for me. Just as I was about to give up I caught sight of the car in front of me; the last three letters on the number plate read: TRY. This was my test, and I passed, I sailed through the journey and went on to experience my first ever ayahuasca ceremony.

Looking back, I can see how 'Mother Aya' begins working as soon as she calls you. She held me back the first time because I was meant to be there when I was... I would not have connected with all the wonderful souls that I did, including Ren, and I would not be writing this right now!

I wrote in my journal after the retreat, 'so blissed and blessed after a powerful, divine weekend, connecting with souls who instantly feel like home; souls who will be etched on my heart forever more. I bow down with gratitude to Madre Aya for showing me love; love withIN and love withOUT as another layer has been shed.'
It could not have been more true!"

Amy

2.0 CEREMONY

The two Peruvian shaman (referred to as maestros by the facilitators) appeared like everyday citizens of South American origin, and arrived at the retreat with the four Pachamama Temple facilitators around 8pm. At 10pm we all got dressed in white clothing, which had been the suggested attire by Mark (but felt a bit 'culty' if I'm honest), and made our way to the yurt in nervous anticipation. Sixteen 'seekers' (including myself) sat in a candle-lit circle in the dark, teak-wooden yurt – some chatting and some silently contemplating and meditating, as the nervous excitement reached a crescendo.

Mark and the facilitators entered the shadowy space and sat down in a semi-circle at the head of the yurt, opposite the door. As the candles flickered orange and red hues over his triangular grey goatee-beard – reflecting in the glass of his black rimmed spectacles, Mark calmly delivered the bad news. The luggage containing the ayahuasca brew had not made it to Mallorca and it was stuck in Barcelona. There was to be no ceremony that night. Patience the lesson no doubt.

Everyone was clearly disappointed including myself, and there was even a moment of despair when I questioned what I was doing there, Maybe I'm not meant to be here doing this? I thought. But our host and the facilitators were optimistic that the luggage would arrive in the morning and the ceremony would go ahead the following afternoon. My moment of despair past, then I knew deep down that it would all work out ok.

As it happened, around 1am, our host poked his shaven head through the doorway into the yurt and informed us that the luggage had arrived at Mallorca's Palma airport and the ceremony would go ahead later that afternoon. I felt relieved and elated, and the energy in the room notably lifted.

Due to the impromptu cancellation, we were offered a free kambo ceremony instead. Kambo is used to reset the body; it comes from the saliva of the Giant Monkey Frog (Phyllomedusa bicolor) found in the Amazon basin, and for many indigenous Amazonian cultures, this purgative, immunity-boosting medicine is very important. Known as the 'vaccine of the forest,' it's gained renown outside of the Amazon as a treatment for chronic pain and drug dependence. Like ayahuasca, kambo is very powerful and shouldn't be administered except under the care of an experienced practitioner, who can help guide people to gain the maximum benefits from its application – helping them to set an intention before the ceremony, ensure proper set and setting during the ceremony, and integrate the experience afterwards.

Research conducted since the 1980's has shown the chemical makeup of kambo to contain short chains of amino acids, known as peptides, which affect gastrointestinal muscles and blood circulation, as well as stimulating the adrenal cortex and pituitary gland in the brain. While there are no clinical studies that definitely back up kambo's efficacy, the properties of kambo peptides make it a promising treatment for conditions such as: depression, migraines, blood circulation problems, Alzheimer's and Parkinson's disease, vascular insufficiency, organ diseases, cancer, fertility problems, deeply rooted toxins, chronic pain, fever, infections, and addiction to opiate or prescription painkillers.

Kambo is traditionally collected early in the morning, when the green, yellow, and blue tree frog from which the venom is derived, are singing, and can easily be found. Without harming them, a shaman scrapes venom from the frog's skin with a stick. The venom is then administered to a person via small holes that are burned into the top few layers of their skin, ideally on the shoulder or somewhere on the top of the arm – close to the heart. Because of its purgative and cleansing properties, kambo is often used as a precursor to an ayahuasca ceremony.

I can attest that undertaking a kambo ceremony was a super-intense experience. In addition to the burning of the skin, it can cause a strong reaction in a person's nervous system, including side effects such as: muscle cramps, swelling, vomiting, and a strong emotional reaction, which is intense in the moment, but leaves people feeling relaxed after about an hour. While the experience is not for everyone, kambo's cleansing effects begin within minutes of administration, and it leaves most people feeling less pain in the days and weeks after treatment.

Our kambo ceremony began around 11pm when we all left the yurt and waited outside in the drizzling rain while Austin (our practitioner who had previously trained with the frog in the Amazon) cleansed and protected the space by performing a ritual with Agua Florida cologne and sage smudging. We then re-entered the yurt one-by-one after Austin had cleansed and protected our bodies and we'd set our intention at the doorway. Mine was to rid my stomach of all the 'badness' and toxicity that many years of active alcoholism and drug abuse must have reeked on my system. As instructed, we then sat in a circle on our mattresses waiting our turn, meditating and attempting to connect with the Spirit of Kampu (the Brazilian Shaman who discovered kambo).

When Austin got around to me, he burned me five times on my upper left arm (down the leg of my tattoo of the Goddess Venus) with a 3mm incense stick. I felt a slight sizzle each time but nothing I would describe as painful. Austin knocked the scars off by hand before he applied the kambo to my wounds. The effect was almost immediate. A tingling and warmth arose through the top of my arms, neck, and chest, then up into my head, which pulsated strongly as the pressure mounted steadily and I began to feel sick.

Austin began his icaro (a medicine song used by shamans in healing ceremonies) and waved his chakapa (a palm frond rubbed and rattled over or near the patient's body by shamans as a rhythm and healing instrument) around my chest, head, and back. Suddenly 'the purge' began. I vomited strenuously and repeatedly into the white plastic bucket directly in front of me, encouraged by Austin and his two co-facilitators.

Having already observed eight of my fellows go through this process over the past hour, I wasn't fearful, but I knew it wasn't going to be a pleasant experience. I reached a point, after what seemed like ten minutes of sporadic vomiting, where I couldn't vomit anymore, and it felt like I would shit my pants if I didn't get to the toilet quickly!

I was helped to my feet by Austin, who handed me over to Mark, who put his arm around my shoulder and accompanied me from the door of the yurt to the bathroom along the 50-yard gravel path, which felt like 500 miles. Shivering in the cold dark night, Mark rubbed my back and offered me words of encouragement. He told me everything would be alright and that I'd feel great soon. I didn't believe him!

We made it to the bathroom just in time. I still felt super groggy following a moment of diarrhoea and five minutes of recovery, and I found it difficult to get back to my feet to meet Mark at the doorway. He accompanied me back up the lantern-lit path, which reminded me of an airport landing strip, back to the yurt, again whispering words of encouragement – assuring me repeatedly how well I was doing.

I sat back down on my mattress, knowing there was more to come. Ten minutes passed, everyone waited in morbid anticipation, then all-of-a-sudden I asserted loudly, "It needs to come out now!"
I immediately vomited violently, over and over into the white plastic bucket, until it was all out, then I declared, "Fuck you frog!"
This triggered rapturous laughter and applause from my audience. I slumped back exhausted and rested on my mattress, as a huge wave of relief washed over me. Thank God that's over, I thought.

It was Luke's turn. I looked at him pitifully and lied when I avowed, "It's not that bad mate." I lay down on my mattress bearing witness to Luke's mini rite-of-passage, warm against the heat from the black metal log fire in the centre of the yurt, feeling deeply drained but profoundly cleansed throughout my body – with a strong sense of achievement. John, who lay on his makeshift bed to my left, had been administered kambo at the same time as me. We exchanged recognition of our ordeal with a glance, a smile, and a fist bump, and we recounted our suffering while observing Luke and another six of our fellows go through the harrowing process – one by one.

In synopsis, it was certainly a community bonding experience, which prepared us for the ayahuasca ceremony and brought us closer together as a group. I felt intimately part of a new tribe.

Around 2am, after all sixteen of us had been through the procedure, the kambo ceremony concluded. We ate vegetable curry and rice in the yurt, served by a lovely helper and masterfully cooked by the chef, then we all settled down to sleep.

2.1 SPIRITUAL MALADY

After five hours, I awoke feeling pretty fresh considering I'd had another broken night's sleep, and I'd gotten up around 5am to make an emergency toilet trip. That morning, I sensed that my insides, from top to toe, had been cleansed from a long-term accumulation of contaminants, which felt fantastic. Three kambo treatments are recommended but once was definitely enough for me!

As the rest of my fellows began to rise, we ate another vegan breakfast of porridge and fruit, and the anxious anticipation once again began to build ahead of the imminent ayahuasca ceremony, which was scheduled for 4pm that afternoon.

In the hours leading up to the ceremony, I sat on my mattress writing notes for my book *Anonymous God*, and caught up on some well needed sleep under my green blanket, which I'd come to love like a pacifier. I lost myself in a dreamy haze, as I re-established my intentions and considered the information that Leanne had given me on our long walk the previous day. She'd informed me that most of my symptoms (restless, irritable, discontent, unable to concentrate for long periods, not remembering the things I've said, and saying things I don't mean) fall under the label of ADHD. She was very knowledgeable on this subject, as her son had been diagnosed with the condition from an early age. Leanne assured me that I'm not a narcissist, as Adele had implied during a recent conversation, and she told me that my ayahuasca experience would likely help me with my issues around selfishness, which I'd always deemed part of my 'spiritual malady' (as outlined in the 'Big Book' *Alcoholics Anonymous*), which is essentially the inability to manage my emotions, and being prone to selfish, self-seeking, fearful, and dishonest behaviours.

Following my conversation with Leanne, I spoke with Luke about ADHD, and he expressed that he wasn't too keen on 'labels.' I disagreed, as I have no issue with labelling myself an alcoholic because it reminds me that I can never drink alcohol safely. I also expressed that I believe every human suffers to a greater or lesser degree with the 'spiritual malady,' as we are all spirits on a human journey and therefore susceptible to spiritual illness in varying degrees. This is not a mainstream belief, however, so I also feel that we need labels to categorise the different variants of spiritual illness. I've since researched ADHD and I certainly suffer with all the symptoms.

Later on, I got changed back into my white linen trousers, white socks, and white t-shirt, and made my way from the bathroom back up the gravel path to the yurt where everyone was settling down in their positions on the mattresses. Austin sat to my left and Mark to his left – next to the doorway, which was covered with a dark grey blanket. Luke sat to my right and John to his right, then Justus, Daran, Amy, Lita, a facilitator, and the two Shaman. To their right was a facilitator, another facilitator (who was directly across from me), Tim, Natasha, Ingrida, Leanne, Lisa, and Angela – who were sitting on the other side of the doorway completing the circle.

A facilitator came to the centre of the yurt and knelt next to the altar, which was covered in burning candles, photographs, and a variety of trinkets and statues. He called us over one by one to bless us ahead of our psychedelic 'journey,' and administer our dose of ayahuasca.

When it was my turn, I walked over and sat down cross-legged in front of the facilitator – a black haired and thick bearded Polish man with a kindly face, who consistently smoked Amazonian tobacco from a pipe (tobacco in its purest form is psychedelic). He poured the syrupy black liquid out of a transparent jam-jar into a small white cup approximately 2 inches wide by 3 inches high. I bowed my head in thanks then lifted the cup to my lips and downed the lot in one gulp. It tasted like a blend of Bovril and Marmite – neither of which I am a fan. I accepted a slice of tangerine to suck-on to mask the taste – offered by one of the shaman from a plate to my right, then I made my way back to my place in the circle and relaxed in meditation until everyone had drank. Roughly fifteen minutes passed before I began to feel the effect of the medicine.

I initially experienced a mild mood lift and a warmth in my head, as my vision blurred marginally and I felt slightly sedated. I sensed my ego defences softening as my sight became hallucinatory – the candles on the wooden alter in the middle of the yurt appeared more luminous and almost holographic, and all the colours emanating from the flames in the dark room were much brighter than before. My vision slowly transitioned from analogue to Super High-Definition, to holographic, then abstract and fractal, then 7-dimensional over the course of the next half-an-hour. Directly across from me, in her white gown and long flowing brown hair, the facilitator's face morphed into that of a goddess – the physical embodiment of 'Mother Ayahuasca,' as I intuitively understood it. As I marvelled at her, 'Mother' asked me in a divinely feminine tone, using my own inner voice as a conduit, "Are you ready?"

2.2 GUILT AND REMORSE

Dread gripped me, as I realised I wasn't ready to surrender! Nausea came over me abruptly, as I struggled with fearful emotions, which began to bubble up from the depths of my stomach through my chest and surfaced in my throat. Images of Adele and her children Isobel and Lillian flashed repeatedly in my mind, swirling around amongst feelings of guilt, remorse, shame, and regret. Tears poured down my face like a waterfall and I sobbed overwhelmingly at our collective loss as a family.

The discomfort reached a crescendo when the emotional pain became almost unbearable – it felt like my solar plexus split in two as I sat upright on my mattress with my chest toward the ceiling. Arching my head skyward I let out a loud groan, then I grabbed the white bucket in front of me and vomited heavily into it. Immediately following 'la purga,' I felt a huge wave of relief, as my ego disintegrated and I sank deep into the oceanic boundlessness of the 'trip.' I felt heavily sedated with my eyes closed, as I experienced repeated visions of Adele and the kids combined with intense feelings of compassion, empathy, and love.

"Hello, how are you? I love you," declared a woman's voice in my mind. "Please don't forget me," She gently pleaded.
This notion surprised me. I queried how I would ever forget this?

As questions arose in my mind, the voice that I presumed to be 'Mother Ayahuasca,' answered instantaneously with an understanding that seemed to come from an eternal place. It was more like a thought exchange and the product of 'oneness' – through which Mother (an emotionally detached super-intelligence), and I, communicated our thoughts and feelings simultaneously.

Mother explained to me, "Adele is your one true soul-mate, you are destined to be together, and her children will forgive you in time... You must be patient."
This was a massive unburdening.

After some time floating in psychedelia, probably half-an-hour, my awareness resurfaced from the depths of my subconscious – back to my physical self, and I let out a huge sigh then rested my head in between my arms on top of my knees, still weeping tears of sadness and joy.

Luke apprehensively asked me if I was ok. I assured him I was, and he gave me a reassuring pat on my right knee with his left hand. I looked down at my own hands; they were independently alive and moving in geometric formations – seeming mechanical and robotic. This didn't freak me out, but rather, prepared me for the next heavy wave of medicine.

I glanced around and admired the magnificently warped psychedelic scenery. I could hardly make out my fellow seekers in the darkness; they had all morphed into a myriad of shapes and colours amidst primal groans, belches, giggles, and vomiting. As I lay back against the wall and closed my eyes, I thought to myself, "this is unreal," then I witnessed my hands disappear like sand flowing in an egg-timer before I sank back into the immeasurable expanse of the trip.

2.3 AMY'S STORY (PART 2)

"My journey with Aya was not as intense as I thought it would be. At the beginning, I was dealing with a lot of egotistical thoughts as I waited for the medicine to 'kick in' – nerves about what might happen, concerns that nothing was happening yet, frustrations at the noises around me, and envy at the seemingly deep and exciting experiences that were going on around me. Why wasn't anything happening to me?

I was crying internally. I thought the medicine wasn't working when in fact it was like Mother had taken my ego and recorded it before playing it back to me at the highest volume. Here you go… if you want love, you've got to get through this first She teased, and then suddenly colours started appearing! Geometric shapes and patterns, rainbows and symbols that I couldn't quite make out.

I kept trying to grasp on to the image, grab hold of the vision but they were slipping away and swirling off too soon. What is this, I thought, I don't understand. As I moved past these flashing displays I came to a standstill. I was in the car park underneath the hospital where my mother had died. It was dark, empty and silent, just like the night she passed. I stood there, waiting, until the concrete underneath me parted and I peered into the underworld, greeted by a seductive goddess glowing purple. I tried to surrender and let the ground take me but I couldn't let go, my ego would not let me.

I went through many different experiences after that but the most significant for me happened right at the end, when the ceremony had closed and members of the group were sharing their stories. I was still 'in the medicine' and I overheard Ren and Luke talking to each other – having already witnessed the strong bond they had, I was smiling at their closeness. Then suddenly I became overwhelmed by their accents, their northern 'twang' enveloping me, wrapping around me like cotton wool, reminding me of my mother's voice and instantly feeling like home. Then a huge rush of pure, intense love entered my body starting at the base of my trunk, and rose up and up, filling me so full that I could not take any more before gushing out of every pore, every cell, every inch of my being. My eyes streaming with tears, love, love, it's all love!

Before I arrived in Mallorca I asked Mother Aya to show me what it feels like to truly love myself, truly, truly love myself and she did. I just had to get my ego in check first!"

Amy

2.4 LOVE, LOVE, LOVE

"Hello, how are you? I love you," asserted Mother. "You've already forgotten me. Please don't forget me. I love you. I want to spend time with you."

Images of my parents flashed in-and-out of my mind amidst vivid multi-coloured sacred geometric patterns – none of which I could focus my attention on for more than a few seconds.

"Your mom LOVES you," insisted Mother tenderly, "Your dad LOVES you."

This illuminating 'light-bulb moment' travelled from my head to my heart. I let out a loud sigh and hugged my legs, as the tears streamed down my cheeks once again. In that moment, self-acceptance was born and simultaneously integrated with a renewed sense of self-worth.

Images of my work colleagues, friends, and family, flashed in and out of my mind.
"They all love you. You are loved," Mother assured me.
A wave of contentment washed through me – from my toes up to the tip of my head and back down to my toes again. I felt peaceful. I felt serene. I felt whole.

"Hello, how are you? I love you. Please don't forget me," Mother whispered, as I bobbed back to the surface of conscious awareness.

Each time I slipped back into the trip, I delved ever deeper, and I had the sense that emotional blockages were being dissolved – like a drain cleaner dissolving scum in clogged drains – so my soul could shine through. It was hugely invigorating and simultaneously exhausting.

"Think, think, think," asserted Mother, "You have to think things through, and consider others, consider the effect you have on others."
It was clearly time to deal with my selfishness.

Mother laughed at me lovingly, "Silly, you don't drop selfishness, you just act the opposite way. Act kindly. Be altruistic. Selfish is not who you are. You are love, and love is an action. Be of service to others. Be love. And don't forget... I love you, please don't forget me."

Mother's words were now repeating like a mantra in my mind, "Hello, how are you? I love you. Please don't forget me... Hello, how are you? I love you. Please don't forget me," as I descended further into limitless ecstasy.

"You've forgotten me again," proclaimed Mother, as I became lucid once more. I chuckled to myself. I had forgotten. Unexpectedly, one of the maestro's began to sing an icaro with his angelic voice and the entire vibe in the yurt transformed from a high mood to one of ecstatic euphoria. Bearing in mind that I'd spent the best part of ten years regularly frequenting hard-house, trance, and techno clubs, the euphoric feelings generated to the sound of the shaman's icaro far exceeded any I'd ever experienced when dancing to electronically-produced tribal drum beats under the influence of enrapturing drugs such as ecstasy and MDMA. I was firmly planted, like a bud in warm, moist psychedelic soil, germinating in the DMT-dimension – where the mesmerising fractals danced in sync to the rhythm of the shaman's icaro, and the nourishing supersonic sounds incubated my flowering soul. To my amazement, the fractals evolved symmetrically in concurrence with my inherent sense of healing like magical, biological alchemy.

To my left, Leanne was being shepherded through what must have been a harrowing period of her journey by two of the facilitators.
"She's giving birth to herself," observed Mother, as Leanne groaned vociferously like a woman deep in the throes of a difficult labour. This intuitively made sense to me, as Leanne had previously disclosed that she is on a shamanic path of rebirth.

2.5 LEANNE'S STORY

"I found myself in Mallorca, Spain for a second time, drawn by a deep-rooted instinct to come back to the medicine. It had been five months since my first two ceremonies and the integration had been intense, challenging, and life-changing.

I arrived a day early due to the only available flights, which gave me time to rest, recuperate, and build strength for transformation. Chatting to the other participants, I realised many of the group had been directly or indirectly impacted by alcoholism or addiction (including myself). I felt there would be much healing in this regard.

We're encouraged to work with an intention for the ceremony and, on the Saturday afternoon, I realised I didn't have one – I'd simply felt the call and life had transpired to get me there. I left the group and wandered down the field to a grassy corner, kicked my socks and shoes off, and planted my feet on the ground. It was raining slightly, and cold, so I pulled my jacket overhead and simply asked out loud, "Why am I here?"

After a few minutes of contemplation, I felt an energy run from the ground, up my feet and through my body. A serene and feminine voice said, "You're here to hold this vibration, the vibration of Pachamama... and ride the wave."

Later, in ceremony, the nerves kicked in while the spaces in the yurt were blocked to keep out the daylight and plough us into darkness. The medicine was distributed and the wait began. I felt nothing from the first cup, much like my first experience. When the second cup was served, I checked in with my gut instinct and took a very small gulp, mindful of the medicine already in my system.

A few minutes later, the maestro appeared in front of me to sing his icaro. Taking a firm hold of my head, with confident eyes and a beaming smile, he began. I journeyed with the sounds, surrendering to their direction and by the time the maestro left me, I was well aware that 'Mother' was beginning to take control.

My body began to move of its own accord, starting at the neck; my head tracing a long, slow, infinity symbol through the air. Then, deep, deep breathing as my torso rotated and a feeling that was both ecstatic and terrifying moved through my body. Having already worked with ayahuasca, I recognised Her and didn't fight the way I had the first time – I 'rode the wave,' as I had been advised by the motherly voice earlier that day.

Soon, I was no longer in the room, but in a realm of vivid patterns, led by the maestro's icaro. I was no longer myself, but a pattern, continually moving and changing with the energy of the room. In that space, it felt like the truth of all existence was a simple pattern and that everything else was a distortion or variation of this one simple truth. I began to laugh wholeheartedly – deep chuckles of absolute bliss and joy. All my stress and worries... what was I thinking? I vowed never to forget this feeling, and I understood what the voice had told me down in the field that day. I was holding the vibration of Pachamama... and it was simply, beautifully, the vibration of JOY."

Leanne

2.6 DOWNLOAD

I became acutely aware that many of my fellow seekers were deep, deep, deep into the medicine, so I allowed myself to drown with them in the vast ocean of universal connectedness. Mother now communicated with me through the shaman's icaro, translating the foreign, rhapsodic words and sounds.

"Remember, remember, remember," she said, "Hello, how are you? I love you, please don't forget me."
The maestro slowed down his lullaby in anticipation... "Are you ready?" Mother asked. "Really, are you ready?" She asked again.

At that moment the rain poured down outside from the heavens above onto the roof of the yurt.
"I adore the sound of the rain," I thought to myself.
"That's me, making it rain, just for you," Mother proclaimed.
"I am in control of everything... Let go... Let go of control. Stop trying to control people, allow them to be free, and don't manipulate anyone. Be honest. Be love," She whispered.
The thought came to me that I do manipulate people for my own gain sometimes and it needed to stop.

I opened my eyes briefly and the scene was stupendously spectacular. It seemed that I was in a completely different dimension – like being in the most elaborate virtual reality; abstract, 7-D, enraptured, primordial. I'd lost all sense of space and time. In a beatific vision, I was at the beginning and the end of everything in the universe simultaneously, peering upward into an infinite, swirling, brilliant light at the centre of it all.

"Now, are you ready?" Mother asked once more.
I was ready.

I gasped in awe then closed my eyes and experienced my physical sense of self, and my ego (the last remaining semblance of 'me') completely dissolve, as I glided gloriously upward into the infinite light of Nirvana and I became one with what I knew to be God.

I was home. Only Love remained. I had ceased to exist. There was no 'I' any longer; only emergence with the 'Great Power of Love' in a tranquil womb-like place, the Great Beyond, where I floated abidingly with no struggle.

You don't have a soul, you are a soul; you have a body, temporarily. I now know that beyond ego-death lies total relief. I floated in bliss for hours... then I was adrift – observing the swirling, wonderful, brilliant divine light of Love with wonder, and feeling God's benevolent energy pulsate in sync with the rhythm of my heartbeat.

Precipitously, the gloriously lit heavens above opened to reveal a neon chasm, shimmering with rapid-fire lightning bolts. Universal wisdom streamed out from the celestial operating system in the form of a binary code – zero's and one's – downloading directly into my mind-computer, and it sounded like a hummingbird flying across the sky, bddddrrrrrrr-r-r-r-r!

The totality of all available knowledge and wisdom, transferred to me in that moment by the universal 'Programmer,' was disseminated by my brain, and the mass of information was summed up by my organic operating system in three simple words: God is Love.

3.0 ILLUMINATION

It's written in *The Tibetan Book Of The Dead* (traditionally believed to be the work of the legendary Indian Buddhist master Padma Sambhava in the 8th century A.D), "Remember the clear light, the pure clear white light, from which everything in the universe comes, to which everything in the universe returns; the original nature of your own mind. The natural state of the universe unmanifest. Let go into the clear light, trust it, merge with it. It is your own true nature, it is home."

Sambhava's poem, which I randomly came across three days after my ayahuasca experience, perfectly captures my profound, life-changing illumination, in which my understanding of my 'self' as a physical entity completely disbanded, and my remaining quintessence merged with the Great Light, as I became one with Source.

I was 'home' in that womb-like place for what felt like an eternity but was actually no more than a couple of hours. As I emerged from the bliss of Samadhi (a state of perfect consciousness where all distinctions between the personal self and the Great Light merge into oneness – with 'sam' meaning together in sanskrit), Mother greeted me affectionately, "Hello, how are you? I love you. Please don't forget me. Remember, remember, remember... Together, together, together... we will change the world."

Prior to my illumination, before the 'download' had occurred, there was a dark element to my trip. Just before I received my revelatory beatific vision, the brilliant colours dancing and swirling systematically inside my mind's eye dulled through hues of dark red, purple, and brown, to a menacing, shining, and shimmering blackness below me. Simultaneously, the mesmerising geometric patterns mutated into what resembled the scales of a serpent, which I (metaphorically) chose to turn away from, as there was a hint of the demonic lurking in the darkness. I felt it was related to my addictions; not something I wished to face on this journey.

There is a reason, however, that Jesus spent 40 days in the desert, and the great shamans of the world go on 'dieta' (isolation diets); they are grappling with the dark impulses that are an integral part of the human psyche – the desire to conquer, dominate, and secure breeding advantage over others. Not everything dark and scary comes from the outside and the darkness doesn't go away if we ignore it.

Evil, The Devil, is actually the ego. The Hebrew word 'Satan,' from the Greek 'Satanas,' means 'adversary – one who plots against another,' or 'the deceiver,' therefore insinuating ego-deception. Satan Is not a particular character but an in-built adversary to personal progress. The more we pretend, therefore, that our ego isn't there, the more it will control us from our subconscious. I believe this is where all obsessive-compulsive behaviours, including substance and behavioural addictions, stem from.

We each have this unconscious aspect to our personality, our 'shadow,' of which we need to become fully aware and take responsibility, to avoid the darkness overriding the light within. We must also protect ourselves by becoming aware of the shadow of our society, as our corrupt civilisation is not currently designed and arranged to support the true nature of mankind. Rather, the individual human being is compromised and transformed into a machine to work for the 'greater good,' as we are convinced through marketing and advertising to serve capitalist ideals.

By acknowledging what is lurking in the darkness with acceptance and forgiveness, we can gain mastery over it. When we cast the light of conscious-awareness into the dark, it becomes illuminated, and we can learn to control and moderate any unhelpful behaviour or bad habit. Awareness is, therefore, the first step to examining our shadow; we must be willing to admit to cravings for power, prestige, sex and money, and be willing to admit that, no matter how temporarily, it feels good to attain those things. This doesn't mean we are a bad person, it just means we are a typical person with typical human desires; we are all a great paradox in the flesh. We can't escape the biological imperatives of our physical body without first accepting that we don't always have purely altruistic motives; the desire to survive and propagate our genetic code is biologically inherent and often overrides more selfless drivers.

One's heart and soul, however, can recognise that these genetic drives can be overcome once we recognise we are all the product of one universal consciousness living out different lives simultaneously. By illuminating the shadow, we can put our heart back in control, and restore agency over the type of person we're going to be from now on. This is a continuous process of awareness, acceptance, and change.

During the retreat, my attention was fully focused on my selfishness and my relationship issues. I therefore had no intention of facing whatever was lurking in the shadows on that particular journey; hence, one might argue, why I haven't dropped my addictive tendencies since returning from Mallorca, if it's even possible to do so?

Undoubtedly, ayahuasca has helped me to face and overcome certain psychopathological issues, but if I'm going to face my deepest, darkest demons, I may have to 'journey' again with the medicine.

A 2012 study by eleven researchers including José Carlos Bouso and Débora González, at The Sant Pau Biomedical Research Institute in Barcelona, Spain, examined 127 people who used ayahuasca at least twice a month for 15 years, and compared these individuals to people who've never taken the substance. After a series of interviews and tests, the researchers concluded that there is, "no evidence of psychological maladjustment, mental health deterioration, or cognitive impairment in the ayahuasca-using group."

In fact, ayahuasca users had lower presence of psychopathological symptoms; they showed lower rates of depression, anxiety, hostility, and negative traits, and they also performed better on neuropsychological tests and psychosocial adaptations, as reflected in their attitudinal traits towards 'Purpose in Life' and 'Subjective Well-Being.' They also scored higher in the spiritual orientation inventory, which covers nine major components including: transcendent dimension, meaning and purpose in life, mission in life, sacredness of life, material values, altruism, idealism, awareness of the tragic, and fruits of spirituality.

The conclusion: ayahuasca users had better general mental health compared to the control group.

3.1 COSMIC JOKE

"Luke is a soul mate, consider him an older brother who will help you become a better parent," stated Mother.
I reached to my right and held Luke's left hand, he squeezed mine tight and we sat back relaxed on our mattresses, holding hands and basking in Divine Love.

"Together, together, together," Mother repeated, "Hello, how are you? I love you. Please don't forget me. Remember, remember, remember... Together, together, together you will change the world... I brought you all here. I made you wait for me. I wanted you all to practice patience and tolerance because you must learn to practice these principles... Now this feels even more special... I love you all. I want to spend time with you, here, together."

Giggles from Angela and Lisa in the darkness to my left rippled outward through the group progressing from laughter to hysterics, as we all simultaneously grasped the hilarity of the situation; one big cosmic joke.

"It's all a joke," Mother announced. "Have fun, be creative, I am. I do this because I can. I'm having fun."
More snickers of realisation came from around the room.
Can they hear what I am hearing? I thought.

Angela let out an enormous belch then purged profoundly into the yellow plastic bucket before her. She then burst out into gleeful, mischievous laughter, which further infected the rest of the group – including myself. I let out a deep, hysterical belly laugh at the profundity and the insanity of it all. I recognised in that moment that the line between enlightenment and insanity is definitely thin.

3.2 ANGELA'S STORY

"I had knowledge of ayahuasca from years back, and I was even offered a ceremony nine years ago but the timing didn't feel right. After my first experience with the medicine I know I did the right thing to hold back, I certainly wasn't ready back then.

I was specifically drawn to this ceremony as it was a traditional setting with Peruvian shaman singing icaro's. I feel a strong past life connection with Peru and I felt this amazing opportunity with them coming to Europe (and therefore so much more accessible), which couldn't be missed.

I arrived with my friend Lisa, who had taken 'Aya' before, which made me feel much more comfortable. With some physical restrictions due to my disability it was good to have her support there.

I was nervous and excited and the medicine started to take hold of me very quickly; I feel this is because my nervous system is compromised due to a neurological condition called CMT which destroys the myelin sheath around the nerves. Firstly, I started to feel waves of energy coming over me and then I saw a Lego ninja woman's face in the chimney of the yurt fire winking at me. That was Mother's way of saying hello and welcome; not what I had expected!

Very soon after, I began to get very distressed with nausea and I couldn't move. I became very frightened and was helped to the toilet, however, I was absolutely fine. I mentioned to the helpers that I was feeling scared and they told me to surrender and trust. Once back in the yurt, I lay on the floor and I surrendered into a thirteen-hour 'journey.'

It was beautifully horrific. I did have visuals, many strange things I didn't quite understand. Every time I tried to make sense of it I felt a wave of nausea coming over me – it felt like layers of my ego were being peeled back. I often say, "She totally thrashed me!"

I had intense physical pain throughout my body. It felt like someone had blown up my root chakra – and not in a pleasant way. I also have scoliosis and have had serious spinal surgery through my childhood. I felt the medicine moving through my spine clearing the trauma. I also felt Her moving through my muscles especially my neck where I have chronic pain. Again, it felt as if She was releasing years of pain from the cells in my body.

I was literally shaking for hours and I could feel her pulsating and vibrating down every nerve in my body. To me it felt like she was knitting the myelin sheath back together, she was literally healing my nerves. I must point out this was extremely painful, probably one of the most difficult challenges I have been through in my life, not just because of the pain and nausea but the sheer length of time I was on my journey with her. I also had terrible pain in my womb area. I happened to be in the later stages of my period and I know that can affect the intensity of ayahuasca. I've been aware before that I can absorb worry from people into my womb area. This felt like huge karmic healing and Mother told me I was carrying energy for people that I needed to release.

One respite from the physical pain was the healing from the shamans and the laughter. At a couple of points, I literally felt overcome by a mischievous Fae (fairy) who just loved to laugh. As I laughed I saw a dark forest where the tress had demonic faces and I just laughed as if to say, "You don't scare me!"
I was laughing in the face of darkness – and it was easy. I felt like I shapeshifted and my voice changed into a very distinctive laugh, it wasn't my voice anymore. It also seemed like the more I laughed the more people began to purge. I myself however didn't. I felt ready to, I wanted to, so I could be free of the nausea, but she wouldn't leave my body. Many say we haven't released if we haven't purged but for me I felt she wanted to stay in my body so she could continue the physical healing. I only felt her energy start to dissipate four days after the ceremony.

I felt so relieved when I started to feel somewhat normal and said I would never do it again. On the plane home though I was already contemplating that I probably would! Mainly because I knew I had received some pretty terrific healing and how could I not what want to do that again? Despite the exchange...

On returning home I was astounded at my next assessment with my physio just a few days later. She was fully aware of where I had been. I was discharged with huge improvements."

ANGELA

3.3 TRIBE

Once the laughter in the yurt had subsided, I asked Austin, sat to my left, if he was ok, as he was doubled over and still seemed deep in his trip.
"I'm good man," he replied, and hugged me affectionately. I turned to my right and gave Luke a massive, long hug.
"I love you brother," I said caringly.
"I love you too bro," he replied.

I was totally at peace, enjoying perfect acceptance of myself, my brothers and sisters all around me, and the world. I knew a phenomenal change had occurred within me and I was overwhelmingly contented. I still felt quite heavily sedated and I was still experiencing auditory hallucinations and sound distortions, but I was coming back from wherever my soul had journeyed to, and my corporeal experience was once again becoming my tangible reality.

I promptly realised that I hadn't been to the toilet for about five hours. I attempted to stand up but I was unsteady on my feet, as I was experiencing disequilibrium from the medicine. I sat back down on the mattress with the intention of gathering myself and re-attempting to stand, but one of the maestro's began another icaro and I was catapulted back into the trip.

"Hello, how are you? I love you. You've forgotten me again... Please don't forget me. I love you," said Mother tenderly.
I noticed the shaman had been working their way around the circle – sat down cross-legged in front of each person – delivering an icaro directly to each individual and now it was my turn.

The shaman sat in front of me dressed in his traditionally embroidered white and blue ceremonial robe and headwear. He performed prayer-like rituals on my hands and over my head, then he began his icaro directed intentionally at me – his voice awed me like a heavenly orchestra. Mother used the divine sound of his voice to communicate her next insight... "I'm going to give you a gift now, for yourself, and for humanity... Are you ready?" She asked.
I was ready.

"Everyone will know that God is Love. Over millennia, the human brain will evolve and you will all be one with God at all times... You will all know this experience at will, by simply going inside, looking within, you will be with God anytime, anywhere... Then everyone will know, as you now know, that God is Love and He loves you all," She said softly.

The shaman then rounded off my personal icaro with what I interpreted as a ceremonial blessing. I thanked him and we laughed with joy in unison before he moved on to face Austin, who welcomed him like a long-lost friend. I ruminated on Mother's insight for some time; the tractor beam of Divine Love pulling us ever closer.

I'd heard that drinking ayahuasca was analogous to ten years of therapy in one night, and I couldn't agree more. I didn't feel in any way like I'd lost my mind. Conversely, I felt that I'd found so much that I'd always been seeking. I smiled to myself and grabbed Luke's hand and gave it a squeeze.

"You must write this all down," said Mother, "Write, write, write... Writing is your life purpose. Writing gives your life meaning... Spread this message of love... God is Love and He loves you... Adele loves you, Lillian and Isobel love you, your parents love you, your friends and family love you... Remember, remember, remember... Together, together, together... Don't be selfish silly, be kind, be loving, be altruistic... I love you. Please don't forget me."

The intense dancing colours and geometric patterns in my mind's eye were dazzling and took my breath away; it seemed that an obscure symbolic language was available to me but just out of reach of my comprehension.

"I've got another gift for you my son," Mother said dotingly. "You must end your current book *Anonymous God* at the moment we met, then tell the story of our union in a new book entitled, *Together*."

Mother then imparted sternly, "Many people will believe you to be mad, they will scorn, they will ridicule, but know that I love you, know that God is Love, and this is your life purpose, to write, write, write."

As I considered how arrogant and egotistical people would presume me to be, a slight pocket of doubt fizzed up from my stomach into my mind. Simultaneously, I innately knew that I had to tell the truth, and capture my experience in my most creative form of expression.

"Don't forget me, I love you. Be true to yourself and love everybody. Every time you get an itchy nose, an upset stomach or cold feet, that is me reminding you that I am here, and I love you... I want to spend time with you, please don't forget me. Don't forget to come home," Mother whispered adoringly.

I blew out an immense sigh of relief, "Holy Mother of God... What the actual fuck!" I exclaimed out loud.
Many of my fellows laughed in unison and appreciation at my sentiment. No doubt they could relate.

I tentatively hauled my body up and steadied myself by holding onto a wooden beam in the roof of the yurt. Placing my trainers on my feet like a small child, and attempting to balance like a baby giraffe on ice-skates, I moved the dark blanket aside from across the doorway and stepped out into the cold Spanish night.

3.4 JESUS, BUDDHA, AND MOSES

The dark velvet sky was half-filled with silver clouds reflecting brilliant white moonlight. My vision was still accentuated and I felt a deep connection to the cosmos. The moon was three-quarters full; it looked stunning against the ebony backdrop laden with crystalline reminders of unlimited universes – twinkling diamonds hovering above the blackness of thick pine forest.

I walked around the back of the yurt and stood peeing into a bush. As I relieved myself, I looked up into the starry sky and Mother pronounced, "This is how Moses felt after I spoke to him through the burning bush… and this is how Buddha felt after he attained enlightenment… Jesus was crucified because he preached the universal message that God is Love; He was willing to die to spread the gospel, and in dying for his conviction, he proved beyond reasonable doubt to so many that he spoke the truth."

I believe ayahuasca is a conduit to discovering that God is no more and no less than the Great Power of Love. What one does with that information, and how one communicates that message, especially taking into consideration the culture of the time, is down to personal interpretation, and marketing and advertising skills.

My approach is this: God is Love, go find out for yourself – however you see fit. If you don't, you might be miserable, and worst-case scenario, you'll live in your own mental hell-prison, like I did for many years. Whether you use ayahuasca or not is up to you, but I can assure you that it works for inducing an undeniable spiritual experience.

"Hello, how are you? I love you. Please don't forget me… Together, together, together… We are all brothers and sisters and God loves you all… Don't forget, I'll keep reminding you… Hello, how are you? I love you… Your cold feet, your itchy nose, your stomach ache… Call on me and I will help you overcome your troubles and your woes… Remember, remember, remember… I want to spend time with you. I love you. I'm always here… The Ten Commandments, The Eight-Fold Path, The Twelve Steps are different paths to the same destination; God/Enlightenment are the same. Just love. Be Love… Plenty of hugs, plenty of kisses, plenty of I love you's… We're not talking about sexual love here – that's for fun – fun with your beloved and fun with those who want to have fun with you… It's all a joke. One big joke. Be joyful. I do this for fun, to be creative. I do it so we can all laugh together – simply because I can, and because I am a Creator… You are a creator – so have fun with it!.. Don't be so serious… Stop trying to be fashionable and 'cool' and just have fun… Give away everything you don't love, that which does not bring you joy, give it all away," Mother gleefully suggested.

I wondered if I would remember any of these lessons and revelations the next day? I contemplated how I regularly have cold feet and occasionally stomach ache, and my nose itches often. I usually go for style over comfort and I suppose being 'cool' was something I'd always aspired to be, but I'd had previous experience of giving away all my unused belongings following a trip to India, and it was a very cathartic experience, which I was keen to repeat.

Mother's mantra was still chanting in my mind, detached from my own thoughts, "Hello, how are you? I love you," on repeat.

I made my way back around the circular yurt and in through the doorway to the dark, primeval domain that felt so much like a warm welcoming home, so full of love. Some of my fellows were still 'journeying' but most were casually sat up on their mattresses whispering to each other and sharing their individual experiences.

I melted back into my position on the mattress between Austin – who was deep in conversation with Mark – and Luke who grinned at me, "You ok bro?" he asked.
"I'm really good brother," I replied.
"Mother told me you're a soul mate – my older brother – and that you'd help me to be a good parent… I definitely connected with you from the moment we met, and I thought to myself, this guy's got something I want, so I hope you don't mind shouldering that responsibility?"
Luke smiled and responded, "Not at all brother, that's really nice, it'd be my honour," then he hugged me and said, "I love you man."
I affirmed, "I love you too."

3.5 LUKE'S STORY

"My personal interest in ayahuasca was that I wanted to dissolve the illusion of who I think I am. I love the way psychedelics sweep aside or tear down our social and emotional barriers and reconnect you to something bigger and more real than yourself – the interconnectedness of EVERYTHING!

I've understood and believed for some time, through intuition and the teachings of philosophers and spiritualists, the concept of 'the mind made self,' created through the conditioning that is my life and the concept that behind all the conditioning and brain chatter, positive and negative, there is a watcher – a consciousness, a space of peaceful clarity. But getting there proves to be a little tricky, and this, for me, is where the psychedelic reboot has become part of my life; lessons of love, acceptance, forgiveness, and everything in between through plant medicines.

This is my ayahuasca experience as I recall it... A Collective nervous anticipation filled the yurt as the ceremony began, the calm presence of the shamans and facilitators assured me and helped settle my fears. My turn came to take the cup and drink, the brew tasted like Molasses; I liked it and grinned. The room fell silent and within half an hour I forgot why I was there... where is there? Oh yes, I remembered I'd taken ayahuasca and it dawned on me the effects were coming on strong and fast. It started to feel uncomfortable, a voice told me to let go, I surrendered and I quickly became energy tripping in the Etheric plane – the cosmos filled my eyes – open or closed it didn't matter, complex patterns and geometry swirled around me interacting and dancing with me.

After the visuals subsided a little, I was aware of a benevolent feminine energy watching me, she slowly revealed herself and began to dance, she permeated my every cell and filled me with love. I became aware of my new brothers and sisters within the ceremony; I could hear their cries and feel their pain and I cried with them, and when they laughed I filled with their joy and joined in with their laughing. The empathy I felt for the people around me was humbling.

The remainder of my experience was spent sitting with clarity of thought I'd never experienced before, questions came to me and were brushed aside with answers instantaneously. I considered what is life but a series of mistakes to learn from? I could see all my faults and mistakes like a mirror had been held up and I was forced to look at myself, which was sometimes painful but I had never felt such focus and contentment before. It was comforting to know that through quietness and reflection all the answers I'll ever need are inside of me.

I think that ayahuasca is a great tool and teacher, although I think the intention of coming to a space (in this case Mark and Lynette's) with an openness and vulnerability and a willingness to share and learn, to sit with friends and talk about our issues in life, and motivating ourselves to move forward, was for me probably the bigger social key and cannot be underestimated. Ayahuasca has been another jigsaw piece to my life learning mission, life hasn't changed but the way I interact with it has."

Luke

4.0 GOD IS LOVE

One of the biggest mistakes I made in the past was believing that love was about finding the right person, when in fact, love is about becoming the right person and demonstrating your love unconditionally. To love unconditionally, however, is difficult. True love really does love without trying to change the other person; I feel that most humans are not very good at it, including myself. According to the Hindu spiritual teacher and proponent of yoga and Vedanta (Hindu philosophy), Swami Sivananda, "Love expects no reward. Love knows no fear. Love divine gives – does not demand. Love thinks no evil; imputes no motive. To love is to share and to serve."

Love, for me, is connection with myself, other beings, and a Higher Power. The demonstration of my love is selfless service; helping others with no thought of praise or reward. Love is, therefore, an action and a feeling. I believe the most important thing in life is to learn how to spread love and share love, and to be able to accept love, and this is something I've been working on since 2010. American poet, author and contemporary Buddhist teacher, Stephen Levine asserted that, "Love is the only rational act," and I'd have to agree.

Without love, we are like frogs with broken legs, birds with broken wings, and dolphins with broken fins. Love is the only way to remain alive after you're dead, as you live-on in people's hearts and minds. We must, therefore, learn to connect with each other and re-connect with ourselves and our Higher Power, or else we risk passing away slowly in separation and isolation from one another; people who become completely isolated tend to die alone. The Great Power of Love is constantly filling us up, which is why we know inherently to love others. When we are disconnected from the Great Power of Love, we can no longer feel love, and we can no longer give out love.

In Twelve Step fellowships, I regularly experience unconditional love, as the idea is to simply help each other to recover. Alcoholics Anonymous Co-Founders Bill Wilson and Dr. Bob Smith were both intelligent, spiritual beings, who spread a message of love. Thankfully, since their deaths, neither have been elevated to the status of 'guru,' which means sobriety remains achievable for all. One might suggest the reason why people join religious groups, and cults, or follow gurus, is because they're not self-accepting, and they need to feel loved and accepted totally, so they search outside of themselves instead of looking within. For the first time in their lives, they experience acceptance and love, and this feeling is therefore worth keeping no matter the cost. One might also suggest that those who are attached to ancient scriptures and the graceful words of gurus are analogous to a person who drinks from a small well at the bottom of their own garden when the drinking water flows freely all around them.

I'm not a religious man, but I take the best from all religions and leave the rest, then I simply by-pass the middle-man; church, temple or synagogue, and go directly to God. Prayer is my way of asking questions and meditation is my way of becoming equanimous enough to receive the answers. Ever since I started practicing prayer and meditation I've gained a sense that God (as I choose to call my Higher Power) is making order out of the chaos.

I believe God is only concerned with the love at the core of my being, and I don't think He's concerned with outer appearances or material satisfactions, as materialism will never satisfy my soul, which is why I believe we have a primal, deep longing for God, for truth, for Love; it's the call of the soul, often the desperate cry of the soul in times of crisis.

4.1 THE GOOD

In the Platonic schools of philosophy, the 'demiurge' is an artisan-like figure responsible for fashioning and maintaining the physical universe. 360 years before the birth of Jesus Christ, in his dialogue entitled *Timaeus*, Plato described the 'dēmiourgos,' which was a common noun meaning 'craftsman,' but gradually came to mean 'producer,' then eventually 'creator.' In most neo-Platonic systems (200 years after the birth of Jesus), the demiurge is considered the fashioner of the universe but is not itself 'The One,' or the 'Form of the Good,' as outlined in his Socratic dialogue *The Republic*.

It seems to me that Plato, over three centuries *before* the birth of Jesus Christ, laid down his metaphysical 'Theory of Forms' (also known as the 'Theory of Ideas'), including his concept of 'God,' based on visionary restructuralisation experiences under the influence of heavy-duty psychedelic brews such as 'kykeon,' which bore the fungal parasite ergot that LSD was later synthesised from by Albert Hoffman. Combined with a monoamine oxidase inhibitor (to enable ingestion), such as the wild plant Syrian Rue (which some historians believe to be the ancient plant medicine 'soma' that is mentioned in a variety of ancient Indo-Iranian texts but whose exact identity has been lost to history), many psychoactive agents – aside from ergot – have been proposed as the significant element of kykeon, such as psychoactive mushrooms, an opioid derived from the poppy, and DMT, which occurs in an abundance of wild plants in the Mediterranean.

Numerous scholars have proposed that the power and longevity of the religious initiations known as the 'Eleusinian Mysteries,' which spanned two millennia and were held each year by the ancient Greeks at the village of Eleusis near Athens – involving visions and conjuring of an afterlife – came from kykeon's functioning as an 'entheogen' (translating to 'God within'). Entheogens are psychedelic medicines that have been used in a ritualised context for thousands of years; an entheogen is any psychoactive substance that induces a spiritual experience and is aimed at spiritual development. The use of 'potions' for magical or religious purposes was relatively common in the ancient world, especially in Greece. The 'initiates,' sensitised by fasting and prepared by preceding ceremonies, were most likely propelled into revelatory mind states with profound spiritual and intellectual ramifications by the powerful psychoactive potions, which is exactly the same process as an ayahuasca ceremony.

Arguably, none of the many excellent and divinely inspired institutions that ancient Athens brought forward have contributed more to the elevation of civilisation – from a barbarous and savage way of life to an educated and refined state – than the Eleusinian Mysteries. From countless initiations, mankind constructed from them the beginnings of civilised life, and gained the ability not only to live happily, but also to die with better hope. The likes of Socrates, Plato, Pythagoras, and Aristotle, who are amongst the most influential figures in western history, were all reportedly engaging in the ritualistic use of psychedelic substances.

Plato's ingestion of psychedelics would account for his suggestion that behind the veil of reality lies the 'truth' in 'Ideas and Geometric Forms,' whereby the 'Form of The Good'

(God) is the superlative. This perfectly adheres to my psychedelic experience with ayahuasca, whereby I was introduced to 'The Form of The Good' before the 'Form of Ideas' was downloaded into my operating system by the 'Craftsman,' or what I now perceive as the 'Programmer,' then de-coded inside my mind-computer before I re-booted with an unshakable understanding that the universe is inherently good, which means we are all inherently good, and 'The Form of the Good' is Love.

Ironically, with the current trending of traditional medicines such as ayahuasca, peyote, and San Pedro across the world, and the rise in popularity of LSD and psilocybin 'microdosing' in California's Silicon Valley, it seems we are now attempting to deconstruct our faltering civilisation and fill the cultural vacuum by re-focusing our creative energies in order to boost innovation and productivity through technological advancement.

LSD makes the brain much more connected and flexible, with the visual cortex connected to every part of the brain. It also decreases blood flow to the brain's 'default mode network,' meaning there is less activity in the area that is activated when the mind is wandering and thinking about one's self and one's emotional state. When using LSD, one therefore becomes less self-obsessed, more compassionate and empathetic, more committed to a task, and outwardly productive, and also more conscientious and truthful – and therefore more loving and kind.

For me, psychedelics are medicines for consciousness and the soul, (which might be the same thing), as I believe consciousness is pure love – the very Source of creation itself.

In my opinion, God is not some separate, superior, and condemning entity that some religious institutions might claim. I have a theory that by believing God is something exterior from yourself, you separate yourself from the Source, and ultimately become a limited being. God, therefore, is a Life Force, a Higher Power, a Divine energy, a frequency that exists within everybody. If you can get in tune with this frequency of Love, you'll beam like the Sun!

My path it now seems, is to continue to spread this ancient yet eternally contemporary message of Love. I appreciate that part of my mission in life is to bring people together. I must therefore learn to use my gift of sensitivity to build cooperation, teach compromise and patience, and be a peacemaker, but I must also learn to balance my unusually sensitive nature, so I don't become hurt or resentful when I'm upset or in pain – like I did when Adele and I broke-up.

4.2 OVERCOMING PAIN

Leaving Adele and the kids was really painful. At first, I felt relief that the pain I was experiencing in the relationship was over, then following a period of avoidance (whereby I refused to think too much about the choices I'd made), the emotional pain came flooding in – in the form of guilt and shame. There's nothing more real than emotional and physical pain. Everyone has pockets of trauma that are activated (most often) in primary attachment relationships. Life, therefore, can be quantified from moment to moment by how much pain we feel – the absence of which tends to induce a level of happiness and joy, or at the least, peace of mind.

However, consider who you'd be if you stopped living life as a product of your pain? Is your story holding you back? Is what you call 'You' simply an amalgamation of behavioural patterns and habits that you've developed to cope with your pain and suffering? Consider, it's only who you think you are that's wounded and hurt and suffering. Your true self, your Devine Soul, beyond the ego, has never been hurt, as it only knows itself in the wholeness of Love. You could awaken to this truth any moment but at the cost of what you've always known, which is scary and prevents most people from letting go. Are you willing to let go of your character identity, your ego, which is no more than an idea, and embrace the universal truth that you are of God, in God?

Like most people, I'm only ever unloving, mean, or unkind to others, when I feel threatened. The problem is, I've felt threatened regularly at different times in my life. This is unfortunately what our culture often does; it threatens us.

There's the threat of being dominated by your partner; the threat of not getting to work on time because there's too much traffic on the roads; the threat of confrontation on the train because too many people are crammed into the carriages; the threat of poverty if one loses their job. When I feel threatened, I start to look out only for myself, and money becomes my God when I'm threatened economically. This is indicative of our capitalist culture; it doesn't make people feel good about themselves, mainly because it teaches the wrong values. We have to be strong enough to teach our children that the culture isn't working, and no longer buy into it ourselves if we're going to change society. I want to teach my children about love rather than individualism and materialism. I believe we must, therefore, work hard at creating our own culture if we wish to be happy, as happiness can't be found in individualism and capitalism alone.

I'm very blessed to be part of a spiritual community where everyone is equal; men and women, black, white, brown, Catholic, Protestant, Buddhist, Islamic, and Jewish. We're all unique, but no-one is better than anyone else – and it really is that way. I suggest you find, or build, a little community with those you love, and those who love you. If we don't love each other, we find ourselves adrift and we become isolated, and ultimately, we die without loving connections. We must be compassionate and take responsibility for each other; only together can we survive and thrive.

Swiss psychologist, Dr. Carl Jung, posited that any person who's reached the age of 40 and doesn't know who they are, where they are, or where they're going in life, can't avoid becoming neurotic to some degree; this is true whether the individual has satisfied their drives for sex, material wealth, and power, or not. Becoming neurotic is no different than becoming fear-ridden, which is why I believe there's such a need for faith in a Higher Power for many people, as faith is the antidote to fear, and faith is the seed of meaning and purpose.

So many people are living meaningless and purposeless lives these days. Most of the time they seem half-asleep, not present for their life – even when they're busy rushing from one task to another, which they deem to be so very important. I believe they're chasing the wrong things; money, prestige, and power, but it's no surprise, as they're conditioned to do so. Not everyone is taught that self-esteem and peace of mind comes from loving others, being part of a community, and creating things that give you purpose, which therefore gives your life meaning.

I'm sure you'll agree that, day-to-day, the pressures of life can be too demanding; it's often like a tension of opposites pulling us one way then another, as we try to live somewhere in the middle, which is difficult at best. The struggle is like an ongoing wrestling match between love and fear, but ultimately, love will always triumph.

5.0 REALITY

During a long day of flights home from Mallorca to Birmingham via Alicante, with many hours to kill in-between, I had time to process my ayahuasca experience by contemplating and writing it all down in my notebook. My lovely friend Pete picked me up at Birmingham Airport and on the drive home I recounted my experience and gave him the message I'd received for him from Mother; that he's moving steadily along the path and he has a solid foundation of faith – from which I can draw inspiration if I choose.

When Pete dropped me off at my house it was almost midnight and I was very tired but still 'buzzing' from the experience, and I wanted to follow Mother's suggestion to get rid of all my material possessions that I don't love. From the boot of my car I grabbed the white Audi golf bag (that I'd always hated), which came free with the car, and gathered up many of my old clothes and unloved possessions, and tucked them inside. I then put the bag back in my boot awaiting the charity shop. I found it difficult parting with my clothing and material possessions because my sense of identity was attached to them. I couldn't bring myself to get rid of everything all in one go but I was happy that I'd made a start, and I know, over time, I'll give away the remaining items. I sat on the end of my bed exhausted, knowing it was time to attempt to sleep, but I felt overwhelmed, and I was slightly fearful of what the next morning might bring.

I woke up in a cold sweat at 6am to the sound of my alarm. Mother's voice immediately greeted me, "Hello, how are you? I love you. Please don't forget me. Remember, remember, remember… Together, together, together," on repeat.

I felt like I'd hardly slept. Fear dawned on me that I might have psychosis due to the voice in my head. I pessimistically thought, "I can't do this – I can't go to work."

I rolled out of my bed and onto my knees and asked God to help me.

"You're ok," whispered my intuitive inner-voice of Love.

"Get up, have a shower, go to work, you'll be fine. I love you," It insisted.

I dragged myself groggily up to my feet, enjoyed a long, hot shower, dressed myself, meditated for fifteen minutes, packed my work bag, jumped in my car, and drove to work listening to Oprah Winfrey interview Actor Ali Macgraw about love and sobriety for her *Supersoul Conversations* podcast. The coincidental subject matter wasn't lost on me. I smiled inwardly.

I arrived at work and was greeted by a colleague, who historically I disliked for various reasons.

"Hello, how are you?" I asked.

"I'm good thanks, how are you?" was the reply.

"I'm good thanks. Have a nice day," I affirmed, and set off up the stairs to my office.

My new-found benevolence towards my colleague wasn't lost on me either.

Later that morning, I logged into my Facebook account and I had a friend request from someone I'd never met – nor had any previous communication with. We had mutual friends from the Ayahuasca Facebook group I belonged to, so I accepted his request and he asked me questions about my experience with the medicine. I gave him a brief synopsis and he was clearly blown away by my story. I explained that Mother had instructed me to write a book about my experience. As the CEO and MD of a web and print media company, he immediately offered to help me out by building me a free website to sell my books. I was floored by his generosity. He explained that he wanted to help people, and he believed that I needed help to disseminate The Great Power of Love's message.

5.1 RECONCILIATION

For the first month after the retreat I was acutely aware of regular synchronistic events; I felt like I was in a 'flow state' (the zone) more often than usual. Extrinsically, everything was the same as it was before drinking ayahuasca, yet intrinsically my perception was different. My attitude towards people and life was much improved. As the days following the retreat went by, the vivid memory of my experience melted away from my conscious awareness. Spiritual experiences don't last – no matter how profound. Mother's voice gradually faded but I remain reminded of Her presence, and I'm often triggered to think, "Hello, how are you? I love you. Please don't forget me," which reminds me to ask The Great Power of Love for help.

The conclusion I've drawn from my experience with the medicine is that it facilitated a deep spiritual experience, which I'll never overlook and I'll always be able to call to mind; I could never forget it. I can now continue with my life knowing absolutely that God is Love, God loves me, my parents love me, Adele and the kids love me, my family and friends love me, my essence is Love, I love all the people in my life, and I can be kind and loving to those I don't know – and even those I don't like – when my ego doesn't get in the way! I'm also happy and comfortable where I am; the grass no longer looks greener elsewhere, as it so often did before my experience with ayahuasca. My pattern has always been to run away from relationships and responsibilities, and for the first time ever in my life that feeling has now gone.

I've not been cured of my alcoholism, and I still have obvious 'addictive tendencies,' such as over-eating sugar, but I'd never want to use alcohol or any others drugs as a means of escape, or to change the way I feel. I'm also different in certain ways; I'm more patient and tolerant; I'm more thoughtful of other people's needs; I genuinely care more; I'm more insightful, talkative, and inquisitive; I feel totally comfortable in my own skin and I therefore rarely experience anxiety, and I look forward to my future with my love – Adele and her children Lillian and Isobel.

It now seems ludicrous to note that prior to my ayahuasca experience, not only did I not love myself, but I didn't feel the love from my parents, my girlfriend, my family, or my friends. Intellectually I knew they loved me, but I couldn't feel it inside – I was blocked from feeling their love. Addiction plunged me into a space that separated me from my friends and family, and from my ability to feel family as family, rather than vehicles for the fulfilment of my cravings. I only realised this *after* I came back to reality from my 'journey.' It was as though one small piece of the jigsaw puzzle of my life had always been missing, of which I was completely unaware, then suddenly that piece was handed to me by Mother and the jigsaw was complete.

I now know that, as a tiny part of the whole picture, I am missed when I don't fully reveal myself. My contribution is greatly needed in the lives of my family and friends. I recognise that I was not showing up fully for my responsibilities or my relationships. I've also learned that we are stronger *together* when we let people into our lives; the needs of one are fulfilled by the strength of another and vice versa. I must stop presenting only smooth polished edges to people, as I so often did, and be willing to let others see my vulnerabilities more often, and enter into theirs, as I often did not; we are bound together more strongly when this happens. In this puzzle we call life, made up of so many individual odd-shaped people-pieces, each piece is equally important. Even in our weakest moments we are all unique and important pieces of the puzzle.

Most importantly, I now love myself in a way that means I want to really take care of my body, mind, and soul, and this means I can be outwardly loving in a way that I wasn't previously capable, as I have more compassion for my brothers and sisters. Following my experience with ayahuasca, my mom expressed that she felt I was, "Fine how I was before," but she was never aware of how I really felt about myself, and I suppose, if the truth be told, neither was I.

Adele and I reconciled on 29th January 2018 – exactly two years to the day from when we met in London (after 24 years since the first time we met).
"Coincidence is God's way of remaining anonymous," according to Albert Einstein.
The reconciliation was emotional. I explained how, at the time that I left, I felt like the situation was harming me, but I'd realised that our difficulties are helping us both to evolve. Indian mystic and guru, Osho said, "Love is a mirror. A real relationship is a mirror in which two lovers see each other's faces and recognise God. It is a path toward God."

I recounted my ayahuasca experience to Adele and told her that I have faith she's my closest soul mate; my 'Twin Flame.' She agreed. We apologised, embraced, told each other we loved each-other, and we both had a feeling of peace and serenity, as forgiveness had set us both free. Adele and I are now working on what American spiritual teacher and author Gary Zukav posited as, "A partnership between equals for the purpose of spiritual growth."

The next day, I rang my 'brother' Luke and shared my good news. He was really pleased for us. The world, and everything in it, felt right.

I now feel safe in the knowledge that God is Love, I am Love, and Love is the greatest thing in the world. I've been blessed with an intrinsic understanding that all is well in this world, and exactly as it's meant to be at all times – even when it's painful. This takes the majority of pressure I create in my mind out of the equation. I continue to ask Love to help and guide my thoughts, words, and actions, and I now go about my days with a new sense of responsibility.

5.2 GOSPEL OF AYAHUASCA

When I recounted my ayahuasca experience to my parents, my dad (who's been sober in recovery since 1991) assured me it was not a relapse in the alcoholic sense, as I hadn't taken an alcoholic drink. We discussed my psychedelic experience and agreed that it's a grey area in terms of drug-use because ayahuasca is a mind-altering substance. However, anti-depressants, anti-anxiety medications, and opiate maintenance drugs, such as Physeptone and Buprenorphine, are all mind-altering and would not be considered a relapse in the alcoholic sense.

Ayahuasca is definitely not a recreational drug like ecstasy or cocaine but it's a drug in the sense that it's a medicine, which has a sedation and psychological effect when ingested. I prefer the term 'medicine' because I feel the term 'drug' is ambiguous and might suggest using narcotics, being drugged, or being poisoned, whereas medicine suggests treatment, prevention, remedy, cure, and healing, which is more appropriate to ayahuasca I believe.

I have no plans to go around preaching the 'Gospel of Ayahuasca,' because frankly, I don't believe it's for everyone. For example, during my trip, Mother told me that Adele has no need to use the medicine because she already has what I was always seeking. She already possesses personal security.

Ayahuasca is a very powerful medicine with the capability of completely disrupting a person's emotional and psychic equilibrium. It only shows people what they need to work on – it's not a fix for all their problems; ayahuasca shouldn't be taken without this in mind. The medicine, I believe, is for those who are spiritually blocked from Love and haven't yet jived with other means of inter-personal connection or therapy.

Taking ayahuasca is religion in its purest sense, as the word 'religion' comes from the Latin 'religio,' which means to connect. For me, it was also, as I've previously mentioned, analogous to ten years of psychotherapy in one six-hour session. There were incredible highs and tumultuous lows, great difficulties and huge benefits to my journey with the medicine, and the immediate aftermath was challenging.

I couldn't summarise my overall experience with ayahuasca any better than these beautiful words from Flora, the facilitator who became the physical embodiment of 'Mother' during my trip...

"It's been a couple of days since the retreat.
I've been waiting for the right words to come up but this time there simply aren't words to describe the Omnipresence of the Divine during those ceremonies.
I think the word 'grateful' works best.
Everything just fell into place, exactly.
Each and every thought vanished in an Ocean of Stillness.
Every question I ever had in my entire life was answered by The Lord Himself.
We gathered in a circle, just as in ancient times, and Light was spread upon those courageous souls that wanted to find their way back 'home' to the Infinite Field of Love.
There is only Love.
All the suffering you are experiencing is God's tool to put you back on track, to reconnect you with Him, with Her, with the infinite Buddha state, with your Perfect Soul.
Do you remember your mission on Earth?

A beautiful pure Light of Grace will shine upon those that can free themselves from fear and step into pure trust, guided by infinite faith in the Devine.
This is the place where the Magic happens.
It happens in a place of pure surrender."

6.0 LESSONS

Once our ayahuasca ceremony came to a natural close, we were all sat relaxing and talking when the helpers arrived again with vats of rice and vegetable curry, which smelled heavenly and tasted even better. Assuaging my hunger was almost a mystical experience in itself, and feeding the tribe was extremely humbling. Taking the role of 'server,' I knelt on the yurt floor, dishing out the food into ceramic bowls with a metal ladle, which was met with appreciation and gratitude – especially from Sam, who I served first. Sam commented that she was usually the server in all aspects of her life, so to be the first served was a blessing. This humbled me and filled my heart with compassion; it was the perfect lesson about the importance of being of service to others, and awareness of how I don't do enough of it!

Psychedelics such as LSD (acid) and psilocybin (magic mushrooms) will, so I'm told, at the least, increase your general self-awareness and your awareness of the world around you, and can also give you profound insights. Ayahuasca, as I can attest, similarly teaches tangible life-lessons and enlightens the 'journeyer' with truths about themselves and about the universe.

Most spiritual/esoteric traditions say the universe emanates from a 'oneness' of all that is, therefore, it's suggested that everything that exists in creation is composed of the same essential material that emanates from a 'Creator.' Science can't currently give us the answer to what began creation but science has so far verified that unexplained 'dark energy' accounts for roughly 70% of the matter in the known universe, with 'dark matter' accounting for 5% and the celestial bodies accounting for the remaining 25%. The discovery of the Higgs boson particle in 2013 verified the existence of the 'Higgs field,' which was the missing part of the Standard Model of particle physics. The Higgs field hypothetically manifests, from potential energy, the property of 'mass' to fundamental particles that interact with it. The Higgs boson, which was sensationally nick-named the 'God Particle,' could therefore, in principle, be a reservoir of energy from which all matter manifests; a 'Creation field' that gives rise to dark energy.

I believe this Creation field could explain the concept of 'God'; our Creator who is commonly referred to as 'Father' because He is the seed of the universe; God is Love and 'Mother Nature' is the incubator of Love – the facilitator of the transformation of Love into physical matter. The female 'being' is a portal between the spiritual realm and the physical realm; she is the only force in the universe powerful enough to navigate and incarnate unborn souls into our world. Mother, therefore, continually births Love into material existence; like the Higgs field, She is magical. God is everything, but without Mother, He is nothing. Without Mother, life would not exist, and Love, therefore, would not manifest without co-creation. This is why, from unconsciousness or sheer rationalism, mankind has always instinctively added divinity to the personal parents; God the Father and Mother the Goddess.

According to Swiss psychiatrist and founder of analytical psychology, Dr. Carl Jung, the 'motherlove,' which should be one of the most moving and unforgettable memories of our lives, and is the mysterious root of all growth and change, means: homecoming, shelter, and the long silence from which everything begins and in which everything ends. Intimately known and yet strange like nature, 'motherlove' shapes your entire life experience, and is your cherished secret. Your mother was the accidental carrier of that great experience, which includes herself and yourself, all of mankind, and indeed the whole of creation. Every mother carries the inborn image of the totality of life – of which we are a tiny, and often helpless, part.

6.1 HUMMINGBIRD

The central characteristic of any profound spiritual experience is that it gives the recipient a new and improved motivation toward betterment out of all proportion to any previous process of discipline, belief, or faith. These experiences don't make us whole at once; they're a rebirth to a fresh and certain opportunity to grow toward emotional and mental wholeness. Founder and executive director of the Multidisciplinary Association for Psychedelic Studies (MAPS), Rick Doblin said, "Psychedelics are not a substitute for faith. They are a door to authentic faith, born of encountering directly the sacred dimension of everyday experience. This is not the only gate to that discovery, but it is the most ancient and universal, and potentially the most accessible to the majority of the human race."

As a result of my spiritual experience with ayahuasca, I've had a growth spurt toward wholeness and I now just hope to be a tiny but integral part of a greater whole (in Twelve Step fellowships and the human race). Prior to this experience, I was intellectually aware of my selfishness and my inability to form deep and lasting, loving connections with other people, and therefore lacking in those areas, but I felt immobilised as to what to do about it. I'd read, and been told, that self-love was the key – I'd even written a chapter about it in my first book, but I didn't feel it like I do today.

Selfishness is the lack of consideration for other people; also known as egotism and self-obsession. Throughout my life, I've had a lack of consideration for others most of the time. I've also been generally more concerned with my own welfare, pleasure, and advantage, regardless of others feelings. This is the opposite of the person I wish to be. I always aim to be selfless and altruistic but I've often fallen short of the mark, as my own desires got in the way. My self-centred approach to life has meant I've struggled to truly connect with more than a handful of people, and I've ended up pushing all those people away at some point – only to pull them back into my life again when I've realised my mistake. Relationships have been a commodity that I used then traded-in when I felt they'd worn out or served their purpose. This has brought me a lot of pain, especially the ending of my friendship with Jonathan, the ending of my marriage to Sally, and the ending of my relationship with Adele.

I've been aware of the need to change for some time, and fortunately, I've now accepted that I must change from what can objectively seem like an almost narcissistic personality to that of an altruistic human being – if I'm going to have a successful relationship with Adele and meaningful friendships, and enjoy peace of mind. I know that my future won't get better by chance, it will only get better by change; ultimately, if a snake doesn't shed its skin, it dies. I don't wish to end up a lonely old man, and I intend to be helpful, kind, and compassionate moving forward; spreading love like a hummingbird spreads pollen.

After the first ceremony at the ayahuasca retreat, I sat in the lounge with some of the other guests explaining how I'd received a 'download' of universal knowledge from 'The Programmer' of the universe. As I explained the sound I'd heard when the information was transferring into my mind, Sam exclaimed, "That's the sound of the hummingbird!"

In Native American cultures, hummingbirds have long been portrayed as healers, light bringers, and helpers from the spirit world, who carry luck, joy, and love to those they encounter. Hummingbirds, therefore, represent the opening of our eyes and hearts to the wonders of the world. Hummingbirds are fascinating little creatures, darting around like tiny nectar hounds, buzzing around windows and delighting children; pollinating flowers that can't be reached by other birds. Legends say that hummingbirds float free of time, carrying our hopes for love, joy, and celebration; a hummingbird's delicate grace reminds us that life is rich, beauty is everywhere, every personal connection has meaning, and that laughter is life's sweetest creation.

6.2 ROUND TWO

Before our second ayahuasca ceremony I thought to myself, "There's no need to take the medicine again," as I'd already received the answers to the questions I came with, and I was a bit scared of going too deep into the psychedelic-wonderland when I knew I'd be leaving Mallorca for home later that day. Luke felt the same, but after a short discussion, we agreed to drink the medicine a second time, to see if there was anything more to learn on this occasion.

Just one third of a cup later and neither of us went anywhere near as deep as the first time. For me it wasn't massively psychedelic. I only purged mildly. I felt warm, calm, and slightly euphoric, and Mother spoke to me softly, "Hello, how are you? I love you. I've missed you. Please don't forget me... I have no more lessons for you my son... I have given you all the information you need... I have shown you everything you need to see... KNOW that God is Love, and KNOW that We love you."

Cutting straight to the nitty gritty, I'm sure some people will say I went to Mallorca, got 'off my head' on drugs, and I simply hallucinated my experiences. In the past, I absolutely loved getting off-my-head, or 'wasted,' on drugs (including alcohol) for over ten years, so I know the difference. I can't prove it, but I know inherently that there was a presence there – I was engaging with something super-intelligent, and it was nothing like being off-my-head on drugs. It was what I was always searching for back then; re-connection. Mother Ayahuasca has helped me see that life is too valuable to be 'wasted' on anything less than happiness and love.

I can also attest that ayahuasca is definitely not addictive. I haven't had any physical cravings for ayahuasca since the retreat, and when I consider drinking ayahuasca again, I think I wouldn't take the medicine unless I was struggling with a specific problem, which I felt couldn't be dealt with by ordinary psychotherapy, or a lifestyle change. I certainly wouldn't drink ayahuasca outside of an official ceremony without a legitimate shaman to conduct it, and I know that drinking the medicine is no walk in the park; it's an extremely challenging experience. I've little doubt that years of psychotherapy would've eventually uncovered the missing piece of the jigsaw puzzle, however, I've no idea if therapy would've so clearly shown me how to place the jigsaw piece back into the puzzle, nor shown me the infinite abyss of Love from whence the puzzle came.

I needed to fix myself, and I needed to speed up the process for the sake of my relationship with Adele, and my own sanity. I got what I needed, as I was ready and willing to learn what Mother taught me, and the time was right. The integration of these lessons has been natural – like a parent has instilled me with security and self-esteem beyond that which I've previously known, but it hasn't been easy changing, as I still have selfish, obsessive-compulsive, and addictive tendencies.

I always prefer a 'quick fix' if one's available to me, but I don't consider ayahuasca to be a quick fix. It's a quick way to get to know yourself more deeply but the hard work started *after* I drank the medicine. It's one thing being taught a lesson and another thing putting it into practice; the realisations had to be made real in my daily life. There are still amends to be made and some bridges may take a long time to repair; all I can do now is be true to myself and carry the Great Power of Love's message to the rest of the world, especially those closest to me.

Prior to the ayahuasca retreat, arguments between Adele and I seemed disastrous, but in hindsight it was necessary for our spiritual growth. Without provoking each other, without seeing ourselves for who we really are, we would've continued living in an illusion and failing to grow soulfully together. I can now see how, following a long game of 'cat and mouse' involving lots of 'emotional shut-downs' and 'silent treatments,' the tension mounted and I eventually withdrew emotionally from the relationship, then I ultimately 'ran away' by leaving. I was convinced it was over, and I couldn't see how we could possibly get back together – without repeating the cycle over and over again.

Adele, on the other hand, being more mentally and emotionally mature than I, had not wanted the relationship to end, and had tried repeatedly to talk and sort things out. Sadly, I deeply wounded her with my words and she stopped trying, then she let me go – knowing that if we were truly meant to be together, I would come back to her. Thanks to 'Mother Ayahuasca,' the shadow of our relationship was revealed to me, and I surrendered to the painful truth. I realised that I'd left Adele to start a new life in search of happiness but I left with a broken heart and a burdened mind, so I took these problems with me rather than facing them in the relationship.

Happiness is not a new home with a new back yard and hopes of greener grass; happiness is something that must be found in my own backyard, in my own heart. After so much anguish, distress, and provocation in our relationship, I opened up to Adele about my old wounds from childhood trauma and my insecurities, and I took responsibility for the harm I caused her and her family. I experienced considerable ego dissolution and soulful expansion when I made my amends to Adele, who simultaneously opened up to me and shared about her own childhood trauma that she'd been working through with a psychotherapist. When we hugged there was a magnetism so strong that it was undeniable our Life-Force is intertwined.

Powerful lessons had been learned about my true nature, and the nature of all humans, during my ayahuasca experience. I was able to express everything I'd learned to Adele and we've since begun to work through our differences. Already the maturity of our relationship has deepened and strengthened, and we've entered a period of soulful reunion.

After drinking one of the most powerful ego-dissolving medicines on the planet, I still have to live in a world that constantly reinforces my ego. I'm trying to be more-open and friendly but in this overcrowded, chaotic civilisation in which we live, it's more difficult than one might think. The ego might be an illusion, or a fictional construct as the Buddhists say, but the sensation of my ego is almost impossible to shake from moment to moment. Ayahuasca, however, is the best ego-reducer and therapy I've so far endured to help me navigate the challenging terrain of day-to-day life and improve my relationships; not only because I've become a better person but mainly because I appreciate Adele and all the inter-personal connections in my life much more than I did previously.

I had to escape my ego to have that realisation, and it was perhaps only possible because a group of like-minded people came together with a shared intention, which created an emotional intensity that's hard to find elsewhere. I was able to completely surrender my ego and abandon my physical body (which I clung to momentarily as the last line of defence) because I trusted every single person in the yurt. I'm very lucky that I experience a similar emotional intensity, oneness, and ego-reduction, regularly in Twelve Step meetings – where my fellows see me, and love me, for exactly who I am.

7.0 ONWARD

In February 2018, I went to a shamanic drumming session in a local village with a couple of my fellows. The shaman gave us instructions to tune into the beat of her drumming and imagine we were in a place in nature where we could go down underneath the surface of the earth to meet one of our animal spirit guides, who would make it known to us who they are. I imagined that I was lay in the warm sea on a Thai beach (one of my favourite memories from my early twenties). I sank deep into the sand and dropped out into a large underground cave. I then walked through the cave and out into a sunlit wood. I saw a number of animals; a badger shuffling into a bush, a snake slither by, a large golden eagle flying overhead, then a small brown deer, who licked me on my face so I knew it was him.

My mind was catapulted back to the previous New Year's Eve (2017), when I'd stopped my car on a country lane on the way home from a Twelve Step meeting. From afar I'd seen something large standing in the darkness at the right-hand side of the road, and as I slowed my car down to a halt, a large brown deer walked across my path, looked at me, then darted off into the woods to my left. It was an enrapturing spiritual moment.

According to the literature provided after the session, "If a deer shows up, it means you've been involved in some aggressive, negative circumstances, and need to seek out safe, nurturing situations and people. More than ever, you need to trust your gut instinct. You're poised for an enticing adventure, one that will take you down many different paths and lead to many important insights. Be gentle with yourself and others."

I related the historical negative circumstances to my break-up with Adele. I related the safe, nurturing circumstances to my upcoming trip to Gran Canaria – to spend time with my Italian friends. I'm definitely looking forward to my enticing adventure with Adele and the kids.

In the second part of the session, we were again instructed to tune into the beat of the shaman's drumming, and imagine we were in a place in nature where we could travel upward into the heavens, where we would meet another spirit guide (not necessarily an animal), who would again make it known who they are. This time, I imagined floating up to the sky on a cloud where I was met by a cartoon figure with spindly green legs, a boiled egg for a head, big black bug eyes, and huge red lips, who laughed at me hysterically. I avoided him and again saw the large golden eagle flying nearby, so I jumped on her back and she flew me down to earth where I felt I wanted to be, grounded. I trundled into the moonlit forest and came face-to-face with a huge black Grizzly Bear, who roared at me to let me know it was him.

According to the literature, "If a bear shows up, it means you must set clear boundaries and don't compromise, even if pressured. Ask for what you want whether or not you feel you'll get it... Get going on that creative project you have in mind. Take some time out from your usual routines and spend some time in solitude. You may be in-need of physical or emotional healing. Be gentle, and show your love to those you're close to. To find answers to your questions, look inside rather than reading or consulting others… Stay grounded no matter what. It's time to bring your dreams and plans to fruition. It's important to trust your instincts. Don't just wait for something to happen; take action now!"

I related the clear boundaries and asking for what I want to mine and Adele's new relationship. I related the creative project to my writing, and I related the time in solitude to living in my own place before moving back in with Adele. I related looking inside for the answers, and staying grounded, to meditation and prayer, and bringing my dreams to fruition is the whole point of writing this book! I'm certainly being gentle to myself, my parents, my friends, Adele and her children – and showering them all with love.

Two days after the drumming session I drove to Adele's house to make my amends to her children, Lillian and Isobel. We sat down in the lounge. I explained to them why I'd left and that I'd made a massive mistake, and that I hoped to come back home and be part of the family again. Nine-year-old Lillian asked me to bring the joy back, and seven-year-old Isobel gave me a card she'd written, which read, 'I hope you will come and bring all the joy back for all of us. I have really missed you so please come back because you always brought a smile to my face, and I wish you never left because we all missed you.'
I assured them that I'd brought a bag full of joy with me and left it in the hallway! The kids laughed. Lillian told me sternly, "This is your last chance! It better not happen again!"

I know absolutely it won't happen again, and I've learned a valuable lesson about forgiveness from Adele and her children. I heard somewhere that nothing affects a child more than the unlived life of a parent, and I certainly don't want to be that person in Lillian and Isobel's lives. I'm therefore proud of myself for having the courage of my convictions by going on the ayahuasca retreat – despite potential backlash from my friends and family.

Later that evening, Isobel came downstairs and asked Adele if she could speak with me in private. We sat on the staircase and Isobel asked me, "Why did you leave?"
I replied, "I was unhappy because your mom and I were arguing all the time. I thought leaving was the right thing to do but I made a big mistake. I love you and I missed you all."
Isobel then asked, "What comes after mistakes?"
I replied, "Apologies."
She then asked, "What comes after apologies?"
I replied, "Forgiveness."
Then Isobel asked, "What comes after forgiveness?"
I responded, "I don't know?"
Isobel asserted, "Friends."

7.1 REIKI

In February 2018, I arrived in Las Palmas, Gran Canaria to spend a week with my 'spiritual family,' the Italians; Helli, Massi, and Lorenzo. Within 24 hours of arriving, as always, the synchronicity was apparent. Helli was recounting a tale from the family's trip to Italy's Lake Como in 2009, whereby she meditated under a Poplar tree and received some spiritual insights that furthered her spiritual awakening. The Poplar tree communicated to her that she should visit a Chestnut tree in Liguria to receive more insights, which she did, and the Chestnut tree suggested she visit an unspecified cave full of crystals, but she'd never followed up this suggestion. The very next day, while sat in a café eating lunch, we randomly got talking to an Italian guy called David on the table next to us. David was on business in Gran Canaria – selling fancy beer pumps – but his main passion in life was promoting tourism through a foundation he'd established in the direction of his home village in Liguria, Italy.

"Maybe we should try and find the crystal caves!" proclaimed Helli after David had departed.

Later that day, Helli was recounting her 'Mary Magdalene story' (featured in my book *Anonymous God*), and I mentioned the new movie Mary Magdalene starring Rooney Mara and Joaquin Phoenix. That night, Helli was listening to 'Om Shanti Music' via YouTube, and the advertisement on the video was for the Mary Magdalene movie, to which Helli smiled at the coincidence.

During my stay, Massi inducted me into Reiki 'Level One' by giving me the 'atonement' and teaching me the various hand positions to perform Reiki on myself and others. I read the 'Reiki manual' to understand how it works, then I started practicing on myself, using the happiness and strength symbols of 'Kariki.' My general stress levels had been quite high, which had manifested in back, neck, and shoulder pain. Massi, a level 3 Reiki 'Master,' worked on my back with a crystal and the results were positive. After one session the pain had decreased by fifty percent, which I thought was quite miraculous. I've since practiced sporadically on myself, and Adele, with beneficial outcomes but it's not my path, as I don't have a passion for it like Twelve Step recovery. However, I feel that Reiki is another viable and useful instrument for physical and emotional healing from pain and suffering, which can bring 'wholeness' to those who feel less than whole through the concentration of universal energy with love.

The best way for me to feel 'whole,' and connected to Love, is to be connected to other people, as God most often speaks to me through people. In fact, I feel that God *is* people and God is the space between us all, as God is everything. What we fail to realise is that we are smack in the middle of the beatific vision already, as God is the only thing that's happening right now.

When I was in Gran Canaria two years earlier, I often felt lonely. I commented to Massi that this time, even though I was spending just as much time alone, I was really enjoying my own company.
"Yes," affirmed Massi, "This is because now, following ayahuasca, you feel whole, you are no longer lacking."

God places in front of me the things I need to work on. When I need to work on my patience, He places slow and rude drivers in front of me; when I need to work on my lust, He places beautiful women in front of me; when I need to ask for help to overcome my fear, He places interview scenarios or group presentations in front of me.

When I was in Gran Canaria, He placed boredom and isolation in front of me, which I accepted, and like all good alchemists, I transformed these symptoms of fear – with my renewed faith – into a newfound sense of security that has not since left me.

7.2 THE AGE OF TRUTH

After my ayahuasca experience, I was presented with a choice: evolve or remain. If I'd chosen to remain unchanged, I believe I would've been presented with the same challenges until I learned from them, until I learned to love myself enough to choose to change. I chose to evolve, and I was reconnected with the Great Power of Love within me. I now have the strength to explore what lies outside my comfort zone, such as dealing with my defensive nature, and my sugar addiction. I've re-awakened my true nature and I'll continue to evolve with Love; I'll progressively become kinder and more loving I believe.

Ayahuasca and other traditional medicines might, therefore, be the missing link that reconnects us all to Love. We are all wandering souls, but many of us are lost, like I've been. Ayahuasca brings us home to ourselves; the benefits of which are so deeply personal that they're immeasurable and unquantifiable. The medicine, used in the correct ceremonial set and setting, feels like something mankind needs and deserves; connection on an interpersonal level with a Higher Power.

In his book, *The Holy Science*, Sri Yukteswar (guru to the famous yogi Paramahansa Yogananda) posits that we are currently in the Bronze Age, which began around 1699 A.D., moving ever closer towards the Age of Truth (Golden Age), which will commence around the year 4099 A.D. At that time, mankind will easily comprehend all universal mysteries – including the mysteries of Spirit. Following my experience with ayahuasca, I agree with Sri Yukteswar that mankind is going through the essential stages towards the ultimate enlightenment of our species. He explained in *The Holy Science* that mankind first sought to establish the fundamental truth of creation, to describe evolution and the involution of the world, then we became eager to realise the three purposes of life: existence, consciousness, and bliss. We then implemented procedures to deal with the method of realising the three purposes of life, such as yoga and meditation, and finally, we've begun to discuss the revelations, which have come to those enlightened beings who've travelled very far inward and reached the destination that we will all one day reach together. Bliss, the 'Kingdom of Heaven,' is within us all, he posits. In other traditions it's called enlightenment, which can't be grasped with the mind – it can only be awakened to; it's a complete change in perception from ordinary egoic consciousness to consciousness of unity and completeness.

Paradoxically, we seek union with a God that we've conceptually created for ourselves, so that 'It' can save us. We seek experiences, we seek one 'high' after another, and we seek enlightenment; seek, seek, seek! The classic irony is this: as long as you seek you will not find. The search itself prevents the 'seeker' from discovering the truth of 'what is,' yet we must first seek in order to realise that what is sought elsewhere is already within, right here, right now.

Will one more teaching ever give you what you believe you lack? Nothing outside of yourself ever can. Where is the seeker? What is it that is sought? You could seek forever, but when you find what you think you've been looking for, you'll discover it is not 'It.' The path to enlightenment, therefore, or becoming a better version of yourself, is an illusion. You're already everything you'll ever be; enlightenment is waking up to this fact. Seeking outside of yourself is a trap, as enlightenment is where you are. Where else could it possibly be?

7.3 ALL THAT MATTERS

Love is the only way to grasp another human being at the innermost core of their personality. By my love, I'm able to recognise Adele's fundamental traits and features and also see more; I see that which is not yet actualised but ought to be, and that which is potential in myself, as Adele is my mirror. Furthermore, I enable Adele to actualise her potentialities, as I am her mirror. By making each other aware of what we can be – and what we should become, we make these potentialities come true for each other by trusting and having faith in our love and each other. Love, therefore, is my master, which means God is my master. When God is my master I'm free; I'm free to accept life on life's terms and forgive all those who trespass against me.

Whether you believe in God or not doesn't matter. What matters is whether you lead a good life and a good life doesn't mean good food, good clothes, good houses, and good cars, it means having good motivations: love, empathy, and compassion, without dogmatism or complicated philosophy; just simply understanding that all humans are your brothers and sisters and we must each respect our collective human rights and dignity. I don't speak with any sense of authority and I'm in no way trying to be a 'spiritual guru.' Find your own path to God I say – although a guru may well be a viable path. I'm not even saying be like me. In fact, I'm saying don't be like me! Be better, don't let you pride get in the way like I often do. Be God-like. Be Love.

In the end it doesn't matter what your body looks like, how successful your career is, how big your house is, how advanced your yoga practice is, or what your bank statement reads – none of the material stuff matters. All that matters is how we behave and how much we love; family, friends, and fellows. Love is all that matters. We must always love the best in others, and never fear the worst. Our purpose on Earth is to love; with love, *together*, we can turn this crazy world around and we can change, grow, and live with equanimity.

Our spiritual development and progress can be accurately measured by our adherence to two standards: humility and responsibility. My ever-deepening humility, accompanied by an ever-greater willingness to accept and act upon my obligations, are touchstones for my spiritual growth; they are the very essence of right being and right doing. We can't hide from the fact that our world is in crisis; polarised politics, failed economies, terrorism, anxiety-crippled younger generations, family breakdown, mental health, addiction, and environmental collapse. We need a solution, which I believe is to *Do What You Can: today*. Work on yourself, so you can help those closest to you. Prepare for great changes and the movements of 'Mother Nature,' as we move toward the 'Age of Truth.'

Traditional medicines are healing and teaching us, and our true voice is emerging from the depths of our souls – overcoming all obstacles. Low self-esteem, which leads to apathy and prevents people from helping others, is one of the most common obstacles that counsellors and therapists deal with day-to-day; it begins very early, during childhood, in the home. The person with a low opinion of themselves has had family and friends who criticised and complained about their failings, and they've expected others to continue that critical pattern. In particular, they expect their partner to pick up where parents or friends left off to continue to remind them of their shortcomings and failures. We must learn to reject negative evaluations and surround ourselves with friends and relatives who see our value and accomplishments; an environment of criticism is very dangerous to one's mental health and can lead to anxiety and depression.

Encouragement and support bring out one's true potential, and even sparks of genius. In my own life, I had the blessing of encouraging parents and an especially admiring grandmother. I remember Gran telling me how clever I was as a small child, and she always praised me for my talents, which planted a seed of confidence that bloomed and has served me well in my adult life. Obviously, I can't change society for the better on my own. I can, however, radically transform my own consciousness, overturning the societal conditioning that limits my true potential, and we can all do this one by one.

Over time, we can change ourselves to the degree that society changes from the inside out – giving birth to a new way of being. Do not, therefore, seek certainty, or your self-esteem, in the eyes of other men or women. Seek impeccability in your own eyes, and when you don't see it in the mirror, seek humility by helping others. "Through love all pain will turn to medicine," said the Sufi mystic, Rumi.

Layers will be shed; you'll experience rage, depression, and anxiety, but you must ride the waves and embrace the transition. Allow these things to exit your system as your ego is dissolved, so that your true self – your soul – can shine through, like it did naturally when you were a young child.

When I asked seven-year-old Isobel if she remembers where she came from before she was born, she whispered, "Yes. God."

And when I asked her what it was like there she replied joyfully, "Fun and full of Love."

And when I asked her what her favourite thing in the world is, she asserted with an angelic smile, "Family."

INDEX

INTRODUCTION

1. https://www.goodreads.com/quotes/523350-if-you-are-depressed-you-are-living-in-the-past
Author: Lao Tzu
Publisher: Taoism

2. Mysticism: A study and an anthology
Author: FC Happold
Publisher: Penguin

O. SUFFERING

1. The Marriage of Heaven and Hell: A Facsimile in Full Color
Author: William Blake
Publisher: Dover Publications Inc.

2. https://www.rythmia.com/location
Author: Rhythmia
Publisher: rythmia.com

3. Creative Evolution
Author: Henri Bergson
Publisher: Digireads.com

4. https://www.thesacredscience.com
Author: The Sacred Science
Publisher: thesacredscience.com

1. PREPARATION

1. podcasts.joerogan.net
Author: The Joe Rogan Experience
Publisher: podcasts.joerogan.net

2. http://www.ayahuasca-info.com/introduction
Author: ayahuasca-info
Publisher: www.ayahuasca-info.com

3. What is Zen?
Author: Alan Watts
Publisher: New World Library

4. https://katukina.com/doc/rape
Author: katukina
Publisher: katukina.com

5. http://www.sensatonics.de/en/shop/shamanic-art-music/ritual-accessories/huaira-sacha-chacapa
Author: sensatonics
Publisher: www.sensatonics.de

2. CEREMONY

1. https://psychedelictimes.com/kambo/
Author: psychedelictimes
Publisher: psychedelictimes.com

2. https://www.mayoclinic.org/diseases-conditions/adult-adhd/symptoms-causes/syc-20350878
Author: mayoclinic
Publisher: www.mayoclinic.org

3. ILLUMINATION

1. The Tibetan Book of the Dead: First Complete Translation
Author: Graham Coleman
Publisher: Penguin

2. The Death of Satan
Author: Andrew Delbanco
Publisher: The Washington Post

3. http://www.beamsandstruts.com/bits-a-pieces/item/750-neuro-huasca
Author: beamsandstruts
Publisher: beamsandstruts.com

4. http://journals.plos.org/plosone/article/authors?id=10.1371/journal.pone.0042421
Author: journals.plos
Publisher: journals.plos.org

5. https://www.soul-herbs.com/ayahuasca-effects/
Author: soul-herbs
Publisher: soul-herbs.com

6. https://www.youtube.com/watch?v=fMyd1QOP3mw
Author: Addiction Specialist Gabor Maté Ventures Outside Western
Publisher: Nature of Things

4. GOD IS LOVE

1. https://www.azquotes.com/quote/564644
Author: Swami Sivananda
Publisher: azquotes.com

2. http://www.greatthoughtstreasury.com/author/stephen-levine
Author: Stephen Levine
Publisher: greatthoughtstreasury.com

3. Timaeus
Author: Plato
Publisher: Penguin

4. The Republic
Author: Plato
Publisher: CreateSpace Independent Publishing Platform

5. https://www.ancient-origins.net/history/eleusinian-psychedelic-rebirth-rites-ancient-greece-making-comeback-009693
Author: ancient-origins
Publisher: ancient-origins.net

6. https://www.wired.com/story/a-microguide-to-microdosing-psychedelic-drugs/
Author: wired
Publisher: wired.com

7. https://en.wikiquote.org/wiki/Carl_Jung
Author: Dr. Carl Jung
Publisher: Wikipedia

5. REALITY

1. Supersoul Conversations podcast
Author: Oprah Winfrey
Publisher: http://www.supersoul.tv

2. https://www.brainyquote.com/quotes/albert_einstein_574924
Author: Albert Einstein
Publisher: brainyquote.com

3. http://www.thelawofattraction.com/twin-flames/
Author: The Law of Attraction
Publisher: thelawofattraction.com

4. https://www.osho.com/iosho/library/read-book/online-library-nobody-phenomenon-germans-fd565b09-652?p=2c38ccd604b194500544e801d739c26d
Author: Osho
Publisher: osho.com

5. Spiritual Partnership: The Journey to Authentic Power
Author: Gary Zukav
Publisher: HarperOne

6. LESSONS

1. https://home.cern/science/physics/higgs-boson
Author: Cern: Accelerating Science
Publisher: home.cern/science

2. https://carljungdepthpsychologysite.blog/2018/09/13/this-is-the-mother-love/#.XH1NSC2cbBl
Author: carljungdepthpsychologysite.blog
Publisher: carljungdepthpsychologysite.blog

3. Manifesting Minds: A Review of Psychedelics in Science, Medicine, Sex, and Spirituality
Author: Rick Doblin Ph.D
Publisher: EVOLVER EDITIONS

4. http://www.ask-angels.com/spiritual-guidance/hummingbird-meaning/
Author: Ask Angels
Publisher: ask-angels.com

5. https://philosophynow.org/issues/97/Is_The_Buddhist_No-Self_Doctrine_Compatible_With_Pursuing_Nirvana
Author: Philosophy Now
Publisher: philosophynow.org

7. ONWARD

1. https://www.imdb.com/title/tt5360996/
Author: IMDB
Publisher: IMDB

3. https://www.reiki.org/faq/learningreiki.html
Author: Reiki.Org
Publisher: reiki.org

4. The Holy Science
Author: Swami Sri Yukteswar
Publisher: Self-Realization Fellowship, U.S

5. https://www.brainyquote.com/quotes/rumi_597891
Author: Rumi
Publisher: brainyquote.com

Visit **www.dwyctoday.com** for more book titles by Ren Koi
and **www.lifeinrecovery.co.uk** for Ren's LiR Podcast #LiRP

DWYCtoday Publishing, Birmingham, United Kingdom. 2019

Printed in Great Britain
by Amazon